MW01292285

BASS FISHING TIPS

5 in 1

All 5 books to make you a better bass fisherman

BASS FISHING TIPS HOW TO FISH A NEW LAKE

Second Edition

ABOUT THIS BOOK

Success is not the key to happiness. Happiness is the key to success. If you love what you are doing, you will be successful.
Albert Schweitzer

Here is one of the genuinely nice bass I caught

Fishing is a passion for most fishermen. There is a special feeling you get when that fish is on the line, a feeling you cannot get many other ways. It is a feeling I will never get tired of. I put this book together because one thing I always hated was going to a lake for the first time and spending a big part of the day learning the lake and learning where the fish should be. Getting ready to fish a new lake has changed a lot in the past 20 years; you can learn most of what you need to know at home before you even get to the lake.

We have access to so much valuable information online. We also now have fantastic ease of communication. These things have made fishing a new lake so much easier and more productive. You can now do tons of research and know where to fish when you get to the lake. So, you do not have to spend valuable fishing time learning the lake after you get there.

Thank you for checking out my book. The tactics and tips throughout this book will make you a better bass fisherman. You will have more fun because you will spend more of your time catching fish, and less time looking for good spots to fish.

There are hundreds of articles written about fishing impoundments on rivers. Most of them are in the Southern States. There are few articles or books written for fishermen who fish in Northern lakes. There are tens of thousands of lakes, and millions of fishermen who fish the lakes across the northern half of the United States. There is also many fisherman fishing in Canada. Many of them are looking for largemouth and smallmouth Bass.

There are many things about catching bass that are the same no matter where you fish for them. Other things are quite different in northern lakes.

In northern natural lakes, we do not have creek channels in most lakes. We also do not have old roadbeds. There are no underwater cliffs or flooded forests, what we have are a lot of quality bass to catch.

The northern natural lakes were formed by glaciers, the bottoms are different. The lakes have sloping bottoms that follow the shoreline. The farther north you go, the lakes change even more. The lakes are deeper and colder, and the bottoms are rocky and not sand or mud. There are still good numbers of nice bass in the far northern lakes. The farther north you go the smallmouth take over. If you have ever caught smallmouth, you know that they are every bit as much or more fun to catch.

Most of us are not tournament fishermen. We cannot go from lake to lake and have all the greatest electronics to use when we are on the water. There is nothing wrong with having the latest electronics. However, it is not what the average fishermen has at their disposal.

I do not know about you, but I cannot afford to spend two to four thousand dollars or more on a depth finder. The side scanning, map and gps units are awesome, but not in my budget.

I have a depth finder which works well, but it is not even in color. It is a black and white screen, and it shows temperature, and it works for locating fish. It has everything I need. I have the Navionics app on my phone so I can look at great detailed lake maps.

You can do a good job of finding and catching fish without the fancy $3,000 color model fish finders. If you use what you have, and you have a plan before you get to the lake, you can out fish most other fisherman.

I have been bass fishing for over 50 years and have caught many fish. Most of my fishing has been in fertile northern lakes. In these lakes, weeds, and other structure visible from the surface are the focus for bass. It helps to be able to see the bottom and the weed lines on the fish finder to get an idea of what structure is there.

I found a great spot on the lake I fish most. This spot has a flat bottom. It is 16 feet deep, with no structure in that area. There is a hump that comes up to 7 feet, the spot is about 20 feet from the outside weed edge.

Most of the time there are fish on and around that hump. They go back and forth from the hump to the weed edge to feed. There always seems to be fish in the area around the hump and the weed line. I would never have found it without the fish finder.

Over the years of Bass fishing, I have caught many other species of fish. Many Northern Pike some walleyes, perch, crappies, sunfish, and even a couple of carp.

The tips and advice in this book are from my years of fishing experience. Along with reading everything I can and watching Bass fishing videos for 50 plus years.

After you read this book and follow the basic ideas, you can go to a new lake and know where to catch Bass. You will be able to attack that lake without blind experimenting. You can also stop wasting hours of valuable fishing time that you could be catching more Bass.

The tactics in this book will also be useful to find new fish places on lakes you fish now. Most of us must work jobs to pay for our fishing, so we do not have a lot of extra time. When you have time to fish and you get on the lake, you want to catch fish; this book will help you do that.

Thanks for downloading my book, enjoy the book and become a better fisherman.

Reviews are especially important in getting books to more people, please go to the **Amazon site to review** the book for me.

Check out my book Bass **fishing spinnerbaits.** This book will help you become a better spinnerbait fisherman.

Also check out my book **on fishing crankbaits** to help you catch more bass with crankbaits.

How to catch more bass on plastic worms.

How to catch more bass on Jigs.

Thanks again for checking out my book.

If you have questions you can contact me at
mailto:steve@stevepease.net

Or visit stevepease.net for other good reads.

TABLE OF CONTENTS

BEFORE YOU GET TO THE LAKE

People who think they know everything are a great annoyance to those of us who do.
Isaac Asimov

One of the biggest ways you can improve your success when going to fish a new lake is to do your homework before you go. You will learn how much unproductive water you can rule out before you even get to the lake. Learning what is going on under the surface, how fish change, and how lakes change will keep you catching fish.

Lake Maps

One of the most important things to do before you go to the lake is to make sure you have a good lake map. There are books that have maps, and there are maps of most lakes you can buy online.

One of the best options for detailed lake maps is **Navionics.** They have an app you can buy for your phone. It is not a cheap app, but if you fish many different lakes, it is well worth it. The maps they have are much more detailed than you can get anywhere else.

If you go to their website, and scroll down to the bottom, you can see maps of lakes that show detail free. This is a great place to start.

Go to the map of the lake you will fish. Look for the points, sharp drop-offs, underwater humps, islands, and weed lines. Bass as most other freshwater fish are structure oriented most of the time.

Furthermore, mark on your map any creeks going in or out of the lake. Mark any bridges or other obvious structures on the lake that will attract fish.

Mark your paper map with the prime spots you find on the lake map. After that go to Google Maps and find the lake in the overhead or bird's eye view. Look at the earth view so you can see the actual picture from the satellite.

While you are on this view, note where the docks are and how big they are. Docks are a key structure; they attract lots of baitfish and thus attract lots of Bass.

Use the cursor to get the GPS coordinates of the points that are good structure points to hold bass. If you have a GPS device, or have GPS on your phone. You can go to the exact place you chose from the coordinates you got from the earth view map.

If your state has a DNR website like Minnesota. Go to that site to find out more useful information on the lake. **The Minnesota lake finder site** has lots of other good information. You see water clarity, what species of fish are prevalent in the lake, if they stock it and when and what they stocked.

The water clarity gives a depth. The lake I am looking at has averaged between 1.2 meters and 2.1 meters over the past 20 years.

Use the water clarity depth along with what you can see on Google maps from the satellite view. With this information, you will have a good idea where the weed lines will be on the lake.

The weed lines in this lake should be around 6 feet deep. We also know the water is clear, about normal for natural lakes in this area.

The main way to find Bass is to follow the food. In natural lakes, we do not have schools of shad swimming in deep water. What most northern bass eat is crayfish, perch, and bluegills.

We know most crayfish are in shallow water. Most bluegills and smaller perch are also near shore, to medium depth water.

The food fish are structure related. Their only defense against becoming lunch is to hide from the Bass in and around structure.

We can assume that most of the Bass in this lake will be in less than 10 feet of water. That is where the food will be. They will hide in the weeds, or outside the edges of the weeds.

The Bass will feed in those areas because that is where the food is. Using the lake maps, google maps, and the DNR site, you can rule out 80% of the water on the lake.

You can tell that most of the lake will not hold bass before you even leave the computer. When the Bass are active and hungry, catching them is easy if they are in the spots they should be.

I have caught several 2 to 4-pound bass with a fish in them that were not even all the way in the stomach. They were still feeding at that point. That is what they do.

One bass I caught had a 7-inch bullhead in him. The bullheads tail was still sticking out of the bass's mouth, and he him my bait anyway.

Local Information

Getting local fishing information is also another great way to find the best places to fish. You can look at fishing report sites that give the weekly fishing report from lakes in the area.

If you look in your area, you will find useful information about recent fish catches. You will also find what depth and cover they are in.

If you have a cabin on a lake, or a lake you fish a lot, the lake association meetings are a wealth of information on your lake.

There is a great site that started in Minnesota, **Outdoor news. They** have fishing reports from several other Northern states and Minnesota.

There are also sites like **Lake State fishing. This site** gets updated by resorts that want people to know where and what fish are active that week. Look for these types of sites in your area.

Another great way to get local information is to call local bait shops. When you call them, do not ask where they are biting. You will get a better response if you ask questions to confirm what you have already determined.

Such as, are the bass hitting off the deep point in the center of the lake still? Or have they moved into the shallower grass and weed beds at the south end of the lake. etc. Try confirming what you have determined in your research.

You can also search Google by typing in the lake name followed by fishing reports. You will pull up information on fishing reports. You will also get information from any fishing tournaments that have taken place on the lake. This is valuable information to know.

The fishing report search will get information from local guides and resorts. These people want you to know where the fish are active. They want to get you to come to their lake. Look through these reports. Read reviews from people that stayed at the resorts or used the guides.

This is a great confidence builder. You can see you figured the lake out without even fishing it yet.

Plan for fishing the lake

Once you gather all this information and mark out the most likely places to be productive on your map. Then you are ready to plan how to fish the lake.

The plan is the key to success on a new lake; do not skip this part if you want to catch lots of bass. When you make your plan, always fish the structure you determine at the shallowest points first. Start shallow and work your way deeper. Shallow fish are more active and easier to catch.

Seasonal considerations

Some things will change depending on the season and where the Bass are in the spawning cycle. In the lakes in the states where I fish, there is an open and closed season for Bass fishing. The season opens in mid-May in Wisconsin and the end of May in Minnesota.

When the Bass season opens, the fish are in the spawn to post spawn condition. The water temperature is in the upper 50's. Bass spawn at around 60 degrees. Fishing then can be unpredictable. I do not recommend you catch Bass off beds, let them spawn first.

After the spawn they will scatter throughout the areas you have determined they will be. In the summer they are in the areas you thought and where there is food and cover.

When fishing in the fall, the Bass will move in tighter to cover areas where the food is hiding, and they will be hungry. Docks are important in the fall.

My brother and I were fishing on Bald Eagle Lake, in the Northeast part of the Twin Cities. It was a chilly, cloudy and a rather windy day a few years ago. The wind was blowing from the northwest, so we were trying to fish on the west side of the lake.

The colder the water, the smaller the bait you should use, and the slower you need to retrieve the bait. You should have 3 or 4 baits you feel will be the ones to use when you get to the lake.

It is a good idea to have spinnerbait, a crankbait or jerk bait, a jig, or a worm, and a topwater bait ready. Lures you determined will be the best.

Sometimes the best bait is not what you think. Start with a bait that will cover a lot of water and see if you can find active and aggressive fish.

The biggest bass I ever caught was on opening day on Lake Elmo. I was out before sunrise; it was foggy and dead calm. We were fishing on the North end of the lake in the flooded timber.

I was using a 6-inch black and gold Rapala, throwing it next to the trees and letting it sit until all the ripples disappear. On one cast, I did this, and then gave it a little twitch and it moved a couple of inches.

I saw a wake coming from over 10 feet away, the bass hit it so hard she came completely out of the water. I kept her for a couple of hours in the live well; I was trying to decide if I should hang her on the wall. She was right under 7 pounds, which is huge on a northern lake. I let her go back to make more bass.

My favorite time to use any top water lure is at sunrise. The water is calm, and it is so much fun when you can see them hit the lure with the force of a torpedo hitting a ship.

WHEN YOU GET
TO THE LAKE

Men and fish are alike. They both get into
trouble when they open their mouths.
~Author Unknown

Here is one my wife caught last season

When you get to the lake, the first thing to do is check the local weather. Weather affects Bass and fishing for them. Look at the weather forecast as late as you can before you arrive, so you will get the most accurate forecast.

Is it going to rain? Will it be windy? What will air temp be? Rain may not be a bad thing. It makes it harder and more uncomfortable to fish, but it can make fishing great.

I was fishing with my brother one day; there was a light steady rain that fell most of the day. We were fishing on one of my favorite lakes in the Northern Twin Cities area.

This lake has a couple of reed beds in about 4 feet of water, and the bottom is all sand.

Over the years, we have caught a few Bass in this reed bed. However, on that day, we were fishing weightless grape strait worms. We were catching a Bass on almost every cast.

They were not huge. Most of them were in the 2 to 2 ½ pound range, but you know how much fun they are to catch. They still fight like mad.

We caught and released over 100 Bass in a matter of about four hours of fishing. We also caught several fish in the flats around the reed beds with deep diving crankbait. We were fishing in about 4 feet of water, bouncing them across the bottom through the sand.

It was a once in a lifetime day of fishing I will never forget. The reason they were all in the reeds is because it was cloudy and rainy. Light levels were low and there were no other boats on the lake, so the fish were active.

I have never repeated that day on any lake. I learned that if you find a reed bed in a sandy part of a lake, and you can fish it in low light, cloudy or rainy weather. You can find a lot of hungry and willing Bass.

If it is windy, there can also be benefits. If there is a wind blowing, the Bass will be on the windy side of structures, instead of the leeward side.

The wind blows the bait fish up against the windy side of the structure.

Look at the lake

Look at the shoreline of the lake. Look for the places you picked out as good fish holding spots. Look for other things you did not see from the map. The shoreline contour will extend into the water. If the shoreline is steep, the drop off will be steep. A flat shoreline will have a shallow drop off.

If you get a chance, drive around in the boat with your map. Look at the places you marked and mark any other potential good spots you see.

Look at all the docks, boat lifts and swimming platforms. Some are better than others but overlook none of them.

Mark any promising weed beds, reed beds or grass beds in the lake. Look over the shoreline; if the shore is steep, the bottom of the lake in front of the steep shore is also likely steeper. Mark these areas.

Use your depth finder to look for weed edges, humps, drop offs, and rocks. Be on the lookout for any other structure that could hold fish.

By the time you finish this, you should have a good idea of 10 or 15 prime spots that should hold fish on the lake.

Using this method gave me another great story about locating Bass. The first time I went to my wife's family cabin, I put my boat in the lake and was heading to the cabin. I had looked at the lake ahead of time and determined where I would like to fish.

I was on the way to the cabin. I went through a narrow part of the lake where points on both sides of the lake, jut out from the shore.

On the west side there is a big area of Lily pads next to 10 feet of water. I stopped at the edge of the pads on the calm side of the point and put on a black spinnerbait.

I made my first cast over to the windy side of the point on the outside edge of the pads. I let it land and started an up and down retrieve along the outside edge of the Lily pads.

A nice 4 plus pound Bass hit it about 5 feet after it entered the water. He was waiting for food to swim by the outside edge of the pads. One of the few times I remember ever catching a Bass on my first cast.

Now we know where, now all we need to do is to determine what lures to use and how to fish them.

LURES TO USE

There will be days when the fishing is better than one's most optimistic forecast, others when it is far worse. Either is a gain over just staying home. ~Roderick Haig-Brown, *Fisherman's Spring*, 1951

We now have a good idea of where the fish will be. Determining, which lures to use depends on the season and weather, but also on you. What are your preferred lures? Your favorite lure will be the lure you are most confident in catching fish with. The

confidence factor can make a big difference in if you catch bass or not.

You do not need to have a boat full of rods, but most Bass fishermen do. I carry 4 or five bass rods. I have 3 or four bait casters and 1 spinning rod. I like to use the more finesse type lures on a spinning rod. I like to use the bait casters for spinner baits, crankbaits, top waters, and spoons.

Most of the lakes I fish are clear water, so when I start out, I rig my bait casters with a white or grape spinner bait. And a crankbait or jerk bait on another one, and a Johnson silver minnow on one, and a swim jig on the last.

I set up the spinning rod with a Green pumpkin worm, or a tube jig, a robo worm or a Texas rigged grape lizard. The colors and the size of the baits can vary depending on the water temp and the color of the water and the cloud cover. I also am ready to put on a topwater frog.

I do not read about a lot of Bass fishermen using a Johnson's Silver Minnow lure. However, over the years it has been a killer lure for me in many situations. It is my favorite lure for fishing medium thick weeds. You can fish it fast or slow, and you can catch Bass and a lot of Pike on it.

One afternoon this past summer we got to the lake at about 3pm. It was Friday afternoon; I unloaded the truck, and I went down to the lake.

I walked out on the dock and took a cast with the Silver Minnow along the front of the dock. On the third cast, I caught a nice Bass in the 3-pound range; I took him off and released him.

2 casts later I caught a 5 ½ pound Pike about 15 feet from where I caught the Bass, all within about 10 minutes.

If you have not used a silver minnow, you should get one and give it a shot. Put a black 6-inch wire leader ahead of the lure if you do not want to lose it to Pike.

In the clear water northern lakes, I like crankbaits and jerk baits that are silver and blue. I also use Silver and black, gold, and black, or pumpkin green.

I have bright-colored ones I use sometimes in darker water. I have a full arsenal of Crankbaits from fat to skinny to jointed, some big, some small.

Try different ones to see what works best in the lake's you fish. If I only had a few, my choice would be a Bomber Long A, silver flash, with black or blue back. A square bill baby bass color and a couple of crayfish colored, a brown one and a red one.

The Mann's 1-minus in chrome blue back is a great crankbait. You can use this bait in a lot of places you cannot fish any other crankbaits, and you will catch Bass and Pike.

This bait will only go to a foot deep. It is great for fishing over the top of weed beds.

Spinner Baits

My most used spinner baits are white with chartreuse or white with green mixed. I also like solid black or solid purple.

I like to use a double willow leaf blade, a willow leaf and a Colorado blade, or a single Colorado. I put a 3- or 4-inch twister tail on the bait also.

Another one that may surprise you as effective is a Johnson Beetle Spin. You can put any trailer on them you want, and they catch fish. I get the regular and the saltwater versions, the saltwater ones are bigger.

I have a bunch of other spinner baits also, like most of you, most of them I do not use often.

I have a book about spinnerbait if you want to learn how to best utilize spinnerbaits for Bass.

Crankbaits

The choice of crank baits depends a lot on where I am fishing and what type of structure I am fishing. If I am fishing flats with or without weeds, I use the Mann's 1 minus, or a crayfish-colored crankbait, or a jerk bait.

Pick a lure you are confident fishing. If you do not have one, get a couple and fish them a lot. Get confident with 1 or 2 and make them your go to crank baits.

When I am fishing on edges of weed lines, I like the bomber long A jointed, the blue back one. I have caught Walleyes, Pike, and Bass on this lure, from the same areas. It is a great lure because it has good action at any speed, fast or slow.

If you get out on a morning when there is not a ripple on the lake, and you are near docks or flooded timber. Try a 6-inch original Rapala, gold belly black back. Cast it out and let it sit, then give it a twitch, and get ready for the strike.

Worms

For worms, there are more colors, shapes, and styles than you can imagine. All will work sometimes. What looks cool to you will not always look good to the Bass. Many fishermen get sucked in by a lure that is a cool looking lure. It may not be what the Bass think is cool.

I have found over the years that the best worms in northern lakes I have fished are a 6-inch grape roboworm. A 6-inch black worm with a twister tail. A senko style worm rigged wacky or Texas rigged, and a Mann's jelly worm in green pumpkin and grape.

I like the Zoom super salt plus centipede in the June bug color, black with green flakes. It is a senko type worm that rigged wacky style is killer.

Get the shortest plastic wire ties you can get in black, put them around the center of your wacky worm. Pull them down snug and cut off the excess. Put your hook through the wire tie and you will not tear up your worms so fast. You can also use the rubber o rings made for this. Use two of them on a worm so you can have the hook perpendicular to the body instead of along the body. You will get more hookups.

I also like the Berkley Havoc style worm; they are like a fat grub with a ribbon tail. They work well for a Carolina rig, and you can fish it faster.

Bass Pro shops tournament series have a lot of nice worms that work well. When I fish a worm normal style Texas rigged, I like a straight tail worm.

Jigs

There is a lot of jigs that work well. One you may have never tried that works great is the Road Runner curly tail jig. It has a twister tail trailer with a jig head and a spinner under the jig. I have caught many species of fish on these jigs, lots of Bass.

It is a great search jig because you can fish it fast or slow and cover a lot of water with it. I like it in black, purple, black, and chartreuse, and white. If you use the 1/8 oz. model, you can catch lots of fish and have a lot of fun.

Regular rubber skirted jigs I prefer are black and blue, black, and green, and brown and green.

My favorite tube jigs are the Zoom super salty tubes in black, purple, and green.

I also carry a full assortment of 3- and 4-inch twister tail grubs in black, purple, and white. They can work for many things. Spinnerbait trailers, extra jig trailers, etc. They are a must have in northern lakes.

HOW TO ATTACK THE LAKE

I am not against golf, since I cannot but suspect it keeps armies of the unworthy from discovering trout... ~Paul O'Neil

It does not get much better than this for relaxation

Now you know what to use. You have a good idea where to fish. The next step is how do we attack the lake and catch the most fish, as quick as we can? Do not move too fast. The structure you fish will hold fish. Make sure you cover it well. Hit every side and edge of the structure. You see lots of fishermen moving along at a good speed with the trolling motor. They hit each structure with one or two casts and move on.

The one piece of advice true in almost all situations is to fish shallow. Fish the structures you can see close to the shore. There will always be bass in the shallows, sometimes way more than you would think.

Most of the bass you will catch in natural lakes will be from right past the outside the weed line to the shore.

If it is early in the morning, and the sun is coming up and the lake is like glass. Head for any flooded timbers, or docks. Start with a floating top water lure around the timber and docks.

As you have noticed, my favorite is a skinny rapala, black and gold, or a 4-inch jerk bait.

Let it sit until the ripples stop, give it a little twitch, let the ripples go away again.

If you do not get a strike, take a couple of quick cranks so it dives, and let it float back to the surface. Do it one more time, then crank it fast back to the boat.

You can get strikes anywhere in the cast. Make sure you stay alert and ready, it can be tough at 4:30 am, but you will catch more if you do.

If it is not calm, head for the points. Start by sitting on the windward side of the point, cast out past the weed line. Start with a mid-diving crankbait, cast up to the weed edge, crank it back to the boat with a crank and pause retrieve.

If you do not get fish on this set up, go to a deep diving crankbait, work it the same way. Try a spinnerbait next, and then a jig bounced down the slope. Next step is to go in closer and throw your spinnerbait and a worm into the weeds on the point.

Do not give up on the point to quick, make sure you cover the whole point with several different lures. Points are one of the top fish producers on any lake so fish the whole point.

If there are no points in the area, head for the weed line and docks. Use a spinnerbait to start and fish each good spot well. Hit the docks near the steep shoreline. Pull up even with the end of the dock so you can cast across the front. Then move out and down along each side with a spinnerbait or a jointed crankbait.

After you try those, throw a wacky rigged worm or jig across the front and down both sides. You should have landed several fish by now. Keep working the structures you found while researching the lake.

All the time you are fishing different structure, keep in mind where the baitfish will be. The food is the key to finding Bass. Structure is important because it is where the food hides. Structure is the grocery store for the Bass.

If you think about where the best place is to catch the most fish of any species, in northern lakes, it is next to the docks. All docks have small bluegills and perch most of the time. Where would you go if that were your food and you wanted to eat?

If you stick to the pre fishing work, you did. And have confidence in your plan, you will be a successful Bass fisherman.

The measure of success is different for everyone. If you are a tournament fisherman, success is winning. If you are a normal fisherman, you get out when you can. Success is being able to get on the water, catch fish, relax, and have fun.

CONCLUSION

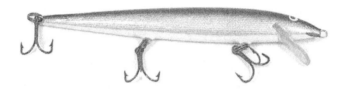

Here is a checklist for researching before and when you get to the water. This will ensure that you have the best fishing possible on that trip.

Before you go to the lake

- Look at lake maps. Printed maps and digital. Check Navionics.
- Have printed maps to mark prime spots
- Check DNR website for more useful information
- Determine where weed lines will be
- Look for fishing catch info on resort sites
- Look for fish catching info on Guide sites and fishing forums

- Call bait shops and resorts to confirm what you have found
- Plan for fishing the lake on a paper map

When you get to the lake

- Check weather conditions for storms and wind
- Look at the shoreline for steep drop offs and points
- Look for visible weed beds from surface
- Confirm your 10 to 15 top spots
- Add any new spots you have found to your map

Attacking the lake

- Start working the marked spots
- Start with ones you think are best because of weather, wind, and time of day
- Use the lures you determined will work
- Focus on shallow water with structure
- Fish good spots with multiple lures

For bass fishing, regardless of if you are fishing in man-made lakes in the south or in the north. Or if you are fishing in northern natural lakes or even rivers, there are 5 key spots that will hold bass.

- **Channel banks** these areas are good on impoundment lakes and rivers. There areas attract bass because they attract bait fish.

- **Rip Rap** Rip rap is also in rivers and impoundments. Impoundments are rivers that have dams to create a lake. The previous channels and creek beds still exist in most of these lakes. Rip rap is a rock wall built up to protect the shoreline from the moving water eroding the shoreline. These rocky areas are a big attractant for crawfish and baitfish. Finding the basses food will always attract bass.

- **Docks** will attract fish in any water. Docks on all lakes and rivers are all going to attract bait fish, which will attract bass.

- **Points** also will be fish attractants in any body of water. Not all points are equal. Having cover at the shore, then dropping into deeper water are the best. Points with docks are the better of two key areas. When you find a dock on a point, make sure you fish every fish holding spot.

- **Isolated cover** can be a fantastic place to find bass. This can be any cover. Always fish docks, weeds, wood, any structure. If you have a weed bed surrounded by sand for a hundred yards, that is a magnet for food, and it will hold bass. If there is a single dock on the shoreline, check it out. This is also good to watch in the spring and fall. If you live where the lakes freeze, people must take docks out for the winter. There may be a single dock left on a busy lake, or the first dock out in the spring. Do not pass up isolated cover.

Thanks for reading my book

If you enjoyed my book and you think this will help you fish a new lake. I would appreciate if you would take a couple of minutes **and go to my page on Amazon and write a review about the book.**

Use your knowledge and, have confidence you know where to fish, and go catch some Bass.

ABOUT ME

My name is Steve Pease. I live in the Northern suburbs of the Twin Cities in Minnesota.

I have been writing for about eight years. I have written several hundred articles for Hub pages and for examiner over the years. For Examiner I wrote a column for the Twin Cities on Disc golf. And one on Cycling in the Twin Cities, and one on Exercise and fitness for the Twin cities.

I write on subjects I am passionate about. Disc golf, exercise, photography, cycling, fishing, and topics that deal with Christian beliefs.

My father is a retired minister, and he has written many books. I have edited many of them and have them available on my site. They cover many topics of interest to Christians today. I have also written an Old Testament trivia book on my own.

I have been playing disc golf since 1978 and love the sport. The greatest thing about disc golf is you can play at any age. At age fifty-nine I am still extremely competitive and beat players much younger than me. Disc golf is a sport you can play at almost any age if you can walk.

I have taken several hundred thousand pictures over the last 35 years. I am always trying to improve my photography. My goal is always to take the best shots I can. I want people to say wow when they look at my shots. I went through the photography course at New

York Institute of photography. It was many years ago, what I learned from the course and my years of experience was worth every dollar.

The key to be a great photographer is to see things that most people do not see, or in a way they did not see it. My favorite types of photography are landscape, portrait, animals, and infrared. I have shot several weddings. I have spent hundreds of hours exploring different places. Always looking for great things to take pictures of.

I have been an avid fisherman since I was a kid. I have had 2 bass fishing boats over the years, but I enjoy fishing for my kayak. I have a sit inside old town kayak, and a sit on top feel free Moken 12 fishing kayak. I also have two old town canoes for going to the boundary waters wilderness area. Or paddling around lakes in my area.

The hardest part about fishing from a kayak is trying to decide what not to take with me. As with most bass fishermen I have tons of equipment, and I always feel I need to take it all with me, in case. Kayak fishing has made me downsize to make everything fit in my kayak.

I spend most of my fishing time catching bass and northern pike. But if I am looking for a good meal, you cannot beat crappies and sunfish. I have spent most of my time fishing freshwater, but I have caught saltwater fish. The biggest was a 380-pound bull shark off Key West Florida in 1985.

I have also loved biking and exercising since I was in my early teens. I like to read nonfiction book so I can keep learning new things all the time. Many of the things I learn I want to share with you and help enrich your life. I want to pass on the knowledge I have learned over the years and share it with others.

Thanks again

Check out my book site for other good books.
Stevepease.net

Bass Fishing Tips for Crankbaits

About This Book

First, I would like to thank you for getting my book. This book is filled with good tips and information that will help you catch more bass on crankbaits. There are thousands of articles out there about how to fish crankbaits. There is more information than anyone could ever use and comprehend or remember. I wanted a book I could read before I went out fishing that would keep the best tips and advice fresh on my mind. That way when I get to the lake, I can have all the best tips ready to use. Therefore, catch the most bass.

Most of us are weekend fisherman. Work interferes with being able to fish every day. Because of that, catching the most bass in the time we can fish, is important. I get that. So, to keep it fresh on your mind you need to go over the information and refresh those ideas. So, when you get on the water, you can focus on catching bass.

This book is my way to do that and share it with other bass fishermen. The purpose of this book is so you can read it before you go out on the lake. That way, you can have all the best tips and advice fresh on your mind. So, when situations come up, you know what to do to catch the most bass that day.

That is why the book is not longer and does not cover all the hundreds of things that it can. This is good concise detailed information you can read before going fishing.

What you will learn from reading this book.

- Why crankbaits catch bass.
- Where to use them in the best situations and locations to catch more Bass.
- What you can do to entice them to strike.

Depending on how you fish crankbaits, you can get reactionary strikes from bass. They may not be hungry. however, are reacting to the bait swimming by. Or they are angry because you are invading their space. You can also get the fish to strike because they are hungry and want to eat the bait.

One of my best bass fishing days ever was when I was fishing with my brother. We were on a little lake outside the Twin Cities. We were fishing in an area that had weeds, but it was a Sandy bottom lake. I threw a little square billed baby bass crankbait. Doing a stop and go retrieve in about 4 to 5 feet of water, and I was catching bass like crazy.

We moved up and down the shoreline of this lake for a few hours. I caught 25 or 30 fish. Nothing huge, they were all in the 2 1/2-to-3-pound range. They were all caught on that one crank bait, fishing in a place where most people would never even try to catch fish.

The point of that story is that sometimes you should try unconventional things. They may be the ticket to having a special fishing day.

Subjects we will cover in this book.

Seasonal fishing

What are the best times and places to use crank baits in the spring, in the summer, and in the fall?

Other weather-related things matter.

What things affect bass fishing and where crankbaits work well in those situations. Cold fronts, warm fronts, approaching storms, and even moon phases can affect fishing.

We also will go over the best places to fish crankbaits and when.

On points, rocks and riprap, weeds, fishing banks, and submerged wood.

We will also cover tactics to help make fishing crank baits better and more effective.

How you should tie on the line.
How to pick the right crank baits
How to pick the right color crankbaits
How you should set the hook when you get a strike.

We will cover the different crank baits

Thin minnow type
Jointed
Top water
Shallow runners
Plug type
Deep divers
Jerk baits
Square bill
Lipless
And the old-style flatfish type crank baits

Where to use each type of crankbait to catch the most bass.

You will learn a variety of retrieves, and which work best in different situations.

Kneel and reel
Reel and kill
Crank and bang
Yo-yo
Bottom bumping
Ripping
Stop and go.
Sweeping
And burn it

We will finish in the last chapter with how to tune your crank bait so it swims the way it should.

Read this book before you go out on the lake and have all these tips and advice fresh in your mind, you will catch more Bass, and you will be a better crank bait fisherman. I know that.

Never forget, it is all about the food for the bass. You find the food they are eating, and you find the bass.

Enjoy the book and be the best bass fisherman you can.

Table of Contents

Seasonal

Spring

The solution to any problem. Work, love, money, whatever, is to go fishing, and the worse the problem, the longer the fishing trip should be.
John Gierach

Bass are very seasonal. Much of what they do is weather related. Water temperature is one of the main controlling things in the life of a bass. Because they are cold-blooded animals, their metabolism, and most things they do change because of water temperature.

Rule of thumb for water temperature.

Cold water = tight wiggle, warmer water = wide wiggle.   Warm water over 60 degrees.

Rat-L-Traps and other lipless crankbaits are good spring baits, because of the tight wiggle action. I like three colors best in spring. Crayfish patterns, firetiger, and chrome with a blue back. The crayfish looks like crayfish. The firetiger looks like a sunfish and a perch, and the chrome blue back looks like a bluegill. If you can determine what the Bass are eating use that pattern to catch more bass. What are the main baitfish the Bass are eating?

A great way to fish crankbaits in the spring is to move your boat in closer to shore. Find where the weeds are growing. They may be only a foot or two high, but any weeds will attract baitfish, and the baitfish will attract the Bass.

Cast up and down the shoreline at the distance from the shore where the weeds are, and fish parallel with the shore. You can keep your lure in the strike zone much longer this way.

Use a lipless crankbait and crank it so it clips the tops of the new weeds all the way back to the boat. Try this technique with a Shad Rap.

Jerk baits and slow fished Shad Raps are great baits for spring. In the cold water, below 50, jerk baits are best fished at low speed.

Once the temperature climbs above 55 degrees, changeover to more traditional crankbaits. Use the shad rap and lipless baits. Jerk baits will still work, but now there are a few more options.

Wired to fish and several top pro Bass fishermen agree. The Rapala Shad Rap is the best cold-water bass fishing crankbait ever made. I have a couple, and I have caught many fish on them. If you have some, do not forget to use them. They are not only for Walleyes.

A Shad rap has a tight wiggle. Most Rapala lures have a tight wiggle because of the narrow-rounded lips. A wider lip will have a wider wiggle.

Another great spring crankbait is a square bill crankbait. A square bill is a great spring crankbait because you can fish over the top of new weed growth. Young weed growth is a magnet for baitfish, which is where the bass will be.

Summer

Crankbaits are great in summer. Because the bass are hunting and on the move. The ability to cover large areas of water in a short time makes finding and catching bass much easier.

Crank baits are as good as spinnerbaits as a search bait. However, you do not see weekend fisherman using crankbaits as much when they are working the banks. The main reason is weeds. Crankbaits are not as weedless as spinnerbaits.

Lipless crankbaits continue to be productive from spring to summer. Try the different retrieves and find what works. Sometimes no rattle works well in cold water. Other times they want all the noise you can make, even in colder water. One of the big advantages to lipless baits is that you can fish them at different depth, on the same cast. This lets you cover a lot of water.

Rat-l-traps are great in summer and spring. You can never go wrong with a chrome body blue back almost any time during the year. That color looks like a bluegill and a shad. Making it work well in northern and southern lakes.

One technique that works great when it is hot is burning a crankbait. Burning a crankbait is what it sounds like, cranking it fast.

The time when this works best is a time you would not have thought it would. Try this technique in shallow water in the middle of the day.

I had an experience in a river with smallmouth bass and pike one summer. I was fishing a small river from shore; I found a deep pool with strong current on both sides of it.

I stood there and cast across the pool. I cranked a black and gold Rapala back as fast as I could crank it, and caught many fish for several days, all day long in that spot.

There are a lot more bass in shallow water all summer long than what most people think. Do not think you have to fish deep to catch big bass.

A perfect example of this is happening as I write this, in the summer. My wife and I have caught 8 bass in the 5-pound range, this summer. All caught in less than 10 feet of water.

Use a steady retrieve with a stop and go every 4 or five cranks of the handle. This technique works; you get their attention when you are in shallow water, you need to check it out.

Fall

The fall crankbait season gets into full swing when the water gets down to the low 60s. It goes until the water temp gets down to around 50.

Many of the techniques and lures you used during the spring will be great again. The main differences in the fall are that you can use bigger baits. You can fish faster because the bass are wanting to eat.

In northern lakes fall can be the best fishing throughout the year for bass. My favorite fall fishing location is docks if the fish are not as aggressive. Cover both sides of the docks and the end with a crankbait, then cover the same area with a swim jig.

Some people take their docks out after Labor Day. That leaves fewer docks to fish, never pass up a dock when fall fishing. I have had fantastic days fishing docks in the fall. Do not stop fishing after Labor Day if you live in the Northern part of the country.

Weather effects on Bass

Wind

I know it is harder to fish this way, but the fish are almost always facing into the current or the way the water is moving. This means you should cast into the wind, so you are retrieving the same direction as the wind is moving the water. This is more important on points.

If you are fishing along a bank that the wind is blowing toward, you should not reel toward the wind movement. There is an option that works well. If you are fishing a windblown bank, and you can get a good position. Move up to the weed line and cast up and down the weed edges.

Lipless baits are easier to fish in a strong wind. They cast better because they have less wind resistance. And they are heavier so you can cast them farther than lighter baits into the wind.

Cold Fronts

If there is a cold front approaching, and you can get out on the water. You may get one of those days you will never forget. Bass can feel the changing pressure and they get active with an approaching cold front and want to eat.

In much of the country, we get cold fronts year-round. They are stronger and have a more drastic effect in the summer months in the Northern states. In Minnesota, we can have strong cold fronts. They can drop the air temperature 20 degrees or more in 15 minutes.

These can be some bad weather days. You can get severe thunderstorms and even tornados, but fishing can be great ahead of the storm. Be careful you do not get caught on the lake during the storm, keep an eye on it and get off the lake before it hits.

After the cold front passes, fishing can be the opposite, fish can turn off, and you cannot get a bite anywhere. The key to finding fish is to slow down and work as close to the cover as you can. Hit the thick cover and you will get more bites.

Isolated cover is always good. If you can find
isolated cover after a cold front, these are
always good areas to fish. Things like stumps
or humps or brush, you can almost guarantee
there will be a bass or 3 sitting there. You must
fish slow and close to the cover.

Conditions after a cold front will be even worse
by having strong winds and a bright blue sky.

Where to fish crankbaits

Points

When fishing points, you want to fish with the
current. Wind is also like current. Because it
moves the water. Position your boat so you can
cast into and retrieve the bait with the wind or
the current if possible.

Bass sit facing into the current. They are
waiting for baitfish to come toward them,
which makes getting food easier.

Taking the wind and weed line into account,
move your boat into the position you think is
the best place to start. Fancast the entire area
before moving. If it is a good point, try a few
different lures as well before you change
position.

When you change position, move to a spot where you can fancast and cover the rest of the point.

Lipless crankbaits are great on points when there is a wind blowing into the point. Ahead of a cold front are the perfect conditions for this area. Make sure you are bumping the bottom or weeds, or any structure on the point as you retrieve the bait.

Rocks

Rocks or rip rap, which are natural or placed by man are both excellent Bass cover. The ones placed by man are there to stop erosion of the soil. These areas can be on rivers or lakes, most natural ones are on rivers.

Never pass one of these areas without fishing it. They are great fish holding structure. Because they attract bait fish into the holes and crevasses where they can hide.

Use a big lipped wide wobbling crankbait you can get down to the bottom. So, it will bounce off the rocks and make lots of noise and commotion to get their attention.

A key spot to focus on is the transition, where the rocks end and the normal bottom starts. On a man-made riprap, there will be a transition; there may not be so much on a natural one.

Weeds

Most people would not think of fishing a crankbait in weeds. I never tried it myself for many years, until I found the bait you can do it with, and it catches fish, Bass and Pike.

The Mann's one minus is a great lure to fish in weed beds. This crankbait dives about 1 foot deep. The chrome with blue back one I use catches bass and pike, and they come up and hit it with a vengeance. My bait has several big teeth marks in it from the pike. Every time I see the teeth marks; it reminds me to not forget to use it because it works.

Lipless crankbaits are also great in weeds. They get hung up less, and if they do, you can rip it loose, and you will get a lot of strikes when you do that.

Banks

Lipless crankbaits are the perfect lure for fishing banks. They are great for ripping through weeds. You can work them down the slope of the bank no matter how deep it goes because they do not float.

If you cast and crank twice fast and pause. Then crank slow until you feel the lure hitting something. Make a couple quicker cranks and pause and let it drop back down. Continue until you are past the strike zone and cast again and repeat.

Submerged wood

Use a square bill bait with a big wide wobble. Cast the bait into the trees and reel at a steady pace. Use the buoyancy of the crankbait to help you keep it from getting snagged. If you feel it get snagged. Stop cranking and point the rod tip at the snag to give it slack, let it float back toward the surface. Wait a few seconds and start the slow retrieve again.

Tactics

Connecting fishing line

For attaching a line to the bait many fishermen only recommend that you tie a loop knot to the crank bait. I am part of a group that does not agree. I like to use a snap swivel on my crankbait line, so I can change lures faster and easier. Many experienced fishermen agree that it does not detract from the lure with a snap attached.

I use green ones on a six-inch steel leader. There are a lot of pike in the lakes I fish, and they like many of the same lures. The fish may see the silver- and brass-colored ones, but I do not think it would make much difference either. Decide on your own. If you are like most bass fisherman, you have 20 or more crankbaits in your box and 5 to 10 that you use. I hate retying every time I want to change.

In the lakes I fish. If I am fishing a shoreline. I can change from an area that one lure is the best to an area where a different one is best. I can change in a couple of minutes; it is easy to change with a snap.

Picking the right bait

Generally, for water clarity. In clear water, use natural colors so the baits blend with the surroundings and look normal to the fish. In dirty or dark water use brighter colors so the fish can see the baits better. Most fish can see good in clear water. If it looks out of place and not normal, it may turn them off instead of attracting them.

The main key to picking the right bait is to find out what the bass are feeding on. Are they feeding on bluegill, perch, sunfish, or crayfish? Match your bait to the food they are looking for.

The second key to picking the right bait is knowing what depth the fish are at. Pro Bass fisherman Mike McClellan says. The foundation of effective crankbait fishing is quite simple. You must know the depth your crankbait is running. If you cannot get the bait to the fish, the color, shape, action, or what model of the lure you have makes no difference.

If your bait is below the fish, there is little chance they will go for it. Mike McClellan also says from his experience the sweet spot is from 2 to 6 feet above the fish. So, if you see fish suspended at 10 feet, start with the bait that runs about 6 to 8 feet deep.

If you do not get a response from that depth, try to go to one that is a little deeper. If you use the bait that runs 10 to 12 feet chances are it will be below the fish, and they will not even see it.

There are a few things other than the actual bait that affects how deep it dives. Line size can make a big difference in diving depth. Also, an untuned bait can have a big effect. Always start with the bait that dives shallower than the fish you are trying to attract. Unless your bottom bumping.

A constant speed retrieve will give you the greatest depth. Use this to figure into your depth choice for your lure. If you are doing a varied speed retrieve, or any stops and starts. Your bait will dive shallower than what it says on the package.

Lure color selection

The first thing to consider is what the fish are eating where you are fishing. Are there a lot of bluegills, crayfish, perch, etc.? Try to match what they are eating. If you are not sure, look around the shallows of the lake.

In most northern lakes, the bass are most likely eating crayfish, bluegills, and perch. Start out with one of those patterns. I have always found that starting with a crayfish or bluegill pattern is a good place to begin.

There are other things to consider for lure color choice. What is the water clarity, weather, and your confidence in the lure? There seems to be an exception to this rule. The firetiger color works great in clear and darker water. Bass love this color pattern. Always try it when you are looking for the right color lure.

All water, even clear water changes the light and makes color less visible, some more than others. Red is the first to disappear under water. That is why many bright red lures work well. Bright red is not a common color in a lake, but as it goes deeper in the water, the red color gets less bright in a hurry.

I have two chrome with blue back rat-l-traps, I use in different water clarity. One is shiny and I use it for darker water, and the other has scales on it which dulls the finish. I use the dull one in clear water.

In muddy or stained water, you want to go with the brighter colors to increase visibility for the fish. Wind and clouds also affect the light penetration into the water. This affects colors you should use. Even clear water has much less light penetration when it is windy and cloudy.

Another rule of thumb that many pros go by is. The colder the water, the darker the colors you use, if everything else is the same.

If the water is clear, and its calm, and the sun is shining, you should use natural colors that look like bait fish on the lake. If any of these things change that causes less light to enter the water, you can change your pattern. Use darker colors and fewer natural colors. Darker colors make a better silhouette against a cloudy sky.

Hook setting

Setting the hook on a crankbait strike should be with a sweeping motion. If you set the hook like you would with a worm or a jig, you have a good chance of jerking the lure right out of the fish's mouth. This is truer with braided line because it does not stretch at all.

Because crankbaits get attacked by bass and pike. A sweeping hook set will drive the hooks in plenty deep and set it solid.

Types of Crankbaits

Thin minnow

If you have access to an inground swimming pool, you should take all your lures there and work them in the pool several times. Look at how each lure works depending on the way you cast and retrieve it. This information is the most valuable piece of information you can have. Knowing how the lure works in the water from the way you retrieve it is crucial. If you can do this, take a day and do it. It will pay off big time on the lake.

The thin minnow lures, like the original Rapala is a shallow to mid running bait. It dives from the surface to around 5 feet deep. You can fish these baits as top water lures also. They are sometimes highly effective but are also great over weed beds and on flats.

Crankbait retrieves with these can cover the entire gamut of retrieves. I have caught fish using a quick crank and stop and let it float back up, all the way to cranking as fast as I could crank it. The thin minnow lures are very versatile and worth using. They have a tight wobble so are good in cold water and warmer water also.

Jointed crankbaits fit into this category also. There are some jointed baits that are not thin minnow type baits. They have several joints and look like real fish. They need to be fished slow to work effectively. They are pricey, I would certainly use a leader with these baits, they are in the $20 and up price range.

The jointed minnows can be a great choice in many situations. If you are fishing waters with lots of fishing pressure. The fish have maybe never seen a jointed lure, so that may give you an advantage.

They are also one of the few baits that work well with a steady retrieve. Because of the extra action from the bait itself. I would still recommend a pause occasionally on a slow retrieve, to get them to strike.

For a minnow type crankbait, they have a much wider wobble, so they are great for warmer water conditions.

They are also great when the fish are less active. You can fish them slow and still get great action from the bait. by jiggling the rod tip on a slow retrieve to give the lure great fish attracting action.

The downside of jointed minnows is they tumble while casting. That sometimes leads to them landing in the water with a hook wrapped around the lure. This means you have a wasted cast and must bring it in and start over.

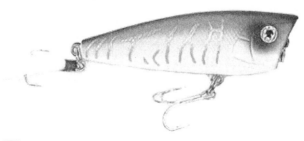

Top water

Thin minnows can also work as a topwater lure if you are fishing structure, and its calm.

I caught my biggest Bass ever using this method. Using a six-inch black and gold original Rapala. Tossing it next to flooded timber and letting the ripples go away, and then giving a slight twitch.

This fish came from quite a way away. I could see the wake on the water, and she came all the way out of the water to take it. She was over 6 pounds, a respectable Bass anywhere, a hog in Minnesota.

There is an entire group of fishing lures that are crankbaits and topwater baits. They are worth looking at and fishing with. One of these lures that have been around for a long time is the Zara Spook.

The Spook and other Chugger type lures are great in the right situation. These lures work best when it is cloudy or when there is a little wind, or other low-light conditions. Particularly early morning and dusk.

There are several other lures that have made a name for themselves in this group. Lures like the Jitterbug, many of them work well. There are also lures that look like bugs, grasshoppers, and bees in this same group.

Another type of bait in this group are the popper lures, ones you let sit and then make them pop and let them sit again. These lures are also best used under the same conditions with good results.

The popper style lures are exciting, the hits can be explosive and lots of fun, stay alert and be ready.

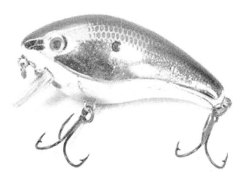

Shallow runner

Square billed crankbaits are shallow runners. However not all shallow runners are square billed baits. The great things about square bill crankbaits are they are fat and short and have a lot of buoyancy. The square bill on the crankbait also makes them get hung up much less often.

You can fish them through areas where you would not fish normal crankbaits. Submerged trees are one of the best places to use them. They also work great anywhere where there is cover. Around docks and even in vegetation they also work well. You will see how weedless they can be.

You want to fish them fast also, you want the fish to be surprised, and have little time to decide, they hit it now or it is gone.

All shallow running baits have a small bill, so they do not dive deep. The bait above is the Mann's 1 minus I love to fish it over weed beds and around docks.

Deep Diver

Deep diving crankbaits are a whole different game. I have one deep diver I use in a variety of places. I use it if I have an area with a sandy bottom, even if it is not deep. I love to drag the deep diver through the sand on the flats, and I catch fish.

There is a lake I fish that has a large area with a bottom like beach sand. There are several docks in this area that hold bass and pike. Dragging that lip, in the sand triggers lots of strikes in that area.

This lure also works great for fishing structure in deeper water. There is a spot I fish, that is in 14 feet of water with a hump that comes up to about 6 feet. I catch bass and walleyes from this hump.

For fishing them in deep water. Al and Ron Lindner have found that a deep diving crankbait takes about 1/3 of the retrieve to get to depth. About 1/3 of it coming back up. This means that if you do not cast long casts. Your bait will never get to the depth you think, and if it does, it is only there for a short time.

Most fishermen have a deep diver or two in their box, but do not use it for fishing deep. In northern lakes, we do not have a lot of deep structure. There are no big schools of suspended Bass to use them on like in southern impoundments.

Paul Elias says most fisherman do not want to spend the energy it takes to fish deep crankbaits. That is true for deep southern impoundments. The conditions exist where that works. It looks like it would be hard work.

He also says it takes lots of work and time to get good at it. It is not so much most fisherman are lazy, it is that they do not want to spend a whole summer learning to do something. It is more of a time thing, most of us cannot fish every day, we must make the best of the time we have.

If you want to do it the way Paul Elias does. here is an article he wrote to go through how to fish the deep structure with crankbaits.

Jerk baits

Good short video about jerk bait fishing

Some people think of jerk baits as their own class of lure. They are crankbaits, but they get fished a different way. Jerk baits come in floating or suspending. The floating ones are thin minnow baits.

The suspending ones are different in that when you stop the retrieve, the bait stays at that depth. The suspending baits are amazingly effective in many situations. To entice bass when they are not aggressive.

The advantage to this is that once the lure is in the strike zone where the fish are, you can keep it there for a long time. It makes it enticing by twitching the rod tip and little sweeps, etc.

Jerk baits are the best choice for spring bass when the water temps are 50 or lower. The keys to fishing in this cold water is patience, it can take up to a couple of minutes per cast in water that cold. A twitch or two and let it sit for up to 30 seconds. Jerk baits can also be amazingly effective when fishing docks. Being able to cast a lure and crank it a couple cranks then stop it and let it sit still is exactly what real baitfish do.

As the water warms, you can fish it faster. A twitching retrieve is highly effective. Cast past the area you think the fish are. Take a couple of hard cranks to get to working depth. Work the lure back with little cranks and lots of rod action. Take pauses in the retrieve also. This keeps the bait in front of the fish for a long time and gets the fish riled until they cannot stand it anymore. Once you are past where you think the fish are, crank it back and do it again.

A short sweeping retrieve is also effective. Start the same way. Cast and make a couple of cranks. Then pause, then sweep the bait a foot and pause again, give it a little twitch, and pause, then sweep it again.

Lipless

One of the best ways to see that a lure is effective is to see how it sells. The Rat-L-trap is the number-one selling lure in the country, and it has been for a long time.

Here is a link to the website with Bill Lewis's story about the birth of the lure. It is a great story because the lure works. I have several, the chrome blue one has worked well for me, also the crayfish red one, and a natural perch looking bait.

The advantages of lipless crankbaits.
- They create a lot of vibration and sound without a lot of drag on the line. The short tilting side to side movement moves a lot of water but are quite weed less because of the design.

- Another advantage is they do not float, so you can fish them at any depth you want. This is a big help in deep water, or clear water with deep weeds.

Lake Itasca in Northern Minnesota is a great example. The start of the Mississippi river is the clearest water I have ever fished. The weeds grow up from the bottom in over 20 feet of water.

Fishing in these weeds is possible with lipless crankbaits. You can cast past the weed edge and let it sink. Then crank it through the weeds and catch fish where it would be extremely hard any other way.

They are often a great choice for checking out flats. You can cover a lot of water fast and pick-up aggressive fish and reaction strikes if you get in their space.

This is also a great way to catch transitioning bass who have spawned and are ready to eat and hunt in the summer.

Cast out and let the bait sink to where it hits the tops of the weeds. Then lift the tip of the rod and start ripping it with a yoyo type retrieve back to the boat. The lack of a lip on the lure makes the fronts smooth and nothing to get hung up on. The hooks should stay behind the lure making the weeds much harder to get on the hooks.

In shallow water, you can crank as soon as the bait hits the water. In mid depth let it sink so it will get down to where the fish are waiting to ambush the food.

Another good retrieve you can use that works great on points and drop offs. Cast it out and let it go to the bottom, when it hits bottom, lift it up a foot or two and let it drop back to the bottom. Repeat a few times. It looks like a wounded or dying fish that is an easy meal.

Lipless baits are also great when fishing into a strong wind. They cast easy for a long way and do not change much in the wind.

Here is a link to a great YouTube video about lipless crankbait fishing. It is a short video with lots of good information.

Square billed

The square bill is cool because you can fish it almost anywhere you can fish a spinnerbait. You can fish it shallow and hit the junk with it. Even bouncing it off the bottom is highly effective in many places. You want to make it hit the structure you are fishing, no matter what it is.

This bait is best in less than 6 feet of water.

Flatfish type baits

This lure is not one you see much anymore, or one you hear much about. This lure is a great lure for smallmouth bass and works fantastic in rivers. I have caught hundreds of smallmouths on this one and an orange one I wore out.

Types of retrieves

If you watch any fishing shows on TV. You notice that the pros do not crank it back at a steady retrieve, most of them are moving the rod while they reel the lure in. What this does is break the flow of the bait, so it is not a continuous motion. To make it look real, you should vary your retrieve.

If you watch fish, even in an aquarium. You see they almost never swim in a straight line and a steady speed from one place to the other. They stop and start, go side to side, even up and down some, seldom a constant speed from one place to the next.

If the bait fish looks injured or is being chased, it is jerkier and erratic in the water. You want to make the bait imitate a real injured fish as much as you can.

Kneel and reel

This retrieve is a retrieve that is to get the absolute most depth out of the lure. You get down on your knees and put your rod tip down in the water and crank it back. You will get an extra 4 to 6 feet of depth.

Reel and Kill

This is the same as the stop and go, but not as rhythmic. You stop every so often and let it sit for a few seconds. The fish hit while it is paused, or when you retrieve it again.

Crank and Bang

This retrieve is about hitting structure with your bait. Some fishermen will untune their crankbaits, so they run to the side. It makes it a lot easier to hit structure by having it run to the side. Have one lure you untune and use in those situations.

Hitting dock posts or hitting trees in flooded timber areas is a great place to do the crank and bang.

A Square lip bait is the best choice for this retrieve. However, any shallow diving bait will work well, all you must do is work on hitting the structure.

Yoyo

This technique is remarkably effective over weed flats that the weeds are below the surface. Or for fishing schooling fish in deeper water. All you do for this one is sink to the proper depth. and lift the rod tip up about a foot then drop it back down and keep doing that throughout the retrieve. This technique is great working lipless crankbaits. It allows you to keep the lure in the fish strike zone for most of the retrieve back to the boat.

Bottom Bumping

This is the technique I use with my deep diver on the sandy flats at one of my favorite local lakes. This lake has sand flats over about 100 acres in 4 to 8 feet of water with reed beds scattered throughout the flats. There are also several good docks in this area. Drag the deep diving crankbait along the bottom. Let the lip dig into the sand. It gets the fishes attention.

Ripping

This retrieve is casting past the weeds and cranking the lure to the weeds. When it gets caught in the weeds, rip the bait free and start again. This retrieve looks like an injured fish and will get Bass and Pike attention in a hurry.

Stop and go

This is what it sounds like. You cast and crank it 3 or four turns and stop. Let it pause for a few seconds and crank it again. The pause and the restart are the trigger that gets the strike.

Sweeping

A sweeping retrieve is like a stop and go retrieve. Except when you move the bait, you sweep it to the side a foot or two, then move it again. Often the sweep will trigger an attack.

Burn it

The burn it retrieves, is the simplest retrieve. You cast the lure out and crank it back at a consistent fast retrieve. This is the no brainer retrieve; anyone can do this. It may be the best under some circumstances, but anyone can catch a fish occasionally with this retrieve.

General Tips

Firetiger is a color that is killer for smallmouths. Northern Pike love the firetiger also.

In most cases the warmer the water, the faster the retrieve. In cold water slow retrieve and pausing will trigger more strikes.

Here is a spreadsheet with a general temperature chart for the best lures.

		BASS LURE TEMPERATURE CHART	
Season	water temp	Clear water	Dark water
Winter	30-40	hair jigs, jigging spoons, grubs	slow spinnerbait, lipless crankbait, jigs
	40-50	jigging spoons, jerk baits, lipless	shallow crankbaits,

		crankbaits, grubs	lipless crankbaits, jigs, spinnerbaits
	50-55	jerk baits, lipless crankbaits, shallow crankbaits	shallow crankbaits, lipless crankbaits, jigs, spinnerbaits
		jigs, slow spinnerbaits	
	55-60	jerk baits, shadraps, spinnerbaits, jigs, buzz baits, swimbaits	Flippin jigs, shallow crankbaits, lipless crankbaits
			spinnerbaits, jigs, lizards
Spring	60-65	jerk baits, lizards, crawfish, tubes, creature jigs, spinnerbaits	spinnerbaits, jigs, crankbaits, buzz baits, worms, grubs

		wide wobble crankbaits, buzz baits, swimbaits	lizards, frogs
	65-70	Topwater, plastics, frogs, jigs, spinnerbaits, crankbaits	plastics, jigs, crankbaits, buzz baits, spinnerbaits, frogs
		Buzz baits, swimbaits	
Summer	70-80+	Topwater, frogs, plastics, deep crankbaits, spinnerbaits, jigs	frogs, buzz baits, shallow crankbaits, spinnerbaits
		Flippin jigs, dropshot, jigging spoons, swimbaits	deep crankbaits, jigs, big worms, other plastics
	75-70	shallow crankbaits, spinnerbaits, jigs,	shallow crankbaits, spinnerbaits,

		smaller worms	jigs, smaller worms
		topwater, buzz baits, frogs	buzz baits, grubs
Fall	70-65	lipless crankbaits, shallow crankbaits, spinnerbaits, jigs	lipless crankbaits, crankbaits, spinnerbaits, jigs
		topwater, worms, drop shot, frogs, buzz baits	worms, frogs, buzz baits
	65-55	buzz baits, shallow crankbaits, jigs, spinnerbaits, swimbaits	buzz baits, spinnerbaits, crankbaits, jigs
		worms	
	55-50	jigging spoons, jigs, spinnerbaits, lipless crankbaits	shallow crankbaits, spinnerbaits, jigs, lipless

			crankbaits
		jerk baits, slower topwater	
	50-	jigging spoons, jigs, spinnerbaits, lipless crankbaits, jerk baits	slow spinnerbaits, crankbaits, jigs

How to tune a crankbait

Sometimes you need to tune a crankbait. Be it from catching a big fish or having it hung up and getting it loose. Other times out of the box they are off. If it is not tuned right it will swim sideways when it is cranked on a steady retrieve. Or it may dart to the side, the problem will get worse the faster you retrieve it.

A miss tuned crankbait will many times flip over if reeled fast.

Check the hook hangers to make sure they are not bent, if one is, straighten it out. If the hook hangers are good, the problem is the pull point where you hook to the line. Bend the tow ring the direction you want the lure to swim. If you break it off it is gone, so be careful. Do it in small increments until it swims straight.

Conclusion

The basics of choosing a crankbait are two things you can observe. Water temperature and water clarity are easy. You can measure the temp and see the clarity. After that you need to make an educated guess on the color and type of crankbait.

Cold-water tight wiggle

Warm water wide wiggle

Crankbaits come in hundreds of combinations of colors. Simplify color selection by matching the color to the water. Dark water starts with darker lures. In clear water use transparent or natural colors that match the lakes baitfish.

General Rules

Be careful, crankbaits are the most dangerous lures you have. They have more hooks per lure, and they are big and sharp. Many people have had crankbait hooks stuck in their body. **Here is a video to get one out if you get hooked.**

Some things you can count on. Fish will move to the side or come up to take a lure. They will seldom go down for it unless you are in shallow water, and it is a worm or a jig. Make sure you are fishing above them and not below them.

If the Bass are not active, it is time to try a different approach. Try wild and erratic retrieves with lots of rod movements and sweeps and pauses. Make sure you are hitting your lure into something.

Picking the depth of a crankbait, choose one that goes deeper than the depth you are wanting to fish. It will only be at the max depth for a short part of the retrieve, and because of other factors will not go as deep as it says.

Try burning it as fast as you can. Try wild colored lures with lots of noise.

You have nothing to lose so see what it takes to get a reaction.

When you are deciding on the right bait, look for natural-looking baits that look like what the fish are feeding on.

Color selection. Use the tip above and think. Colder water uses darker colors with a tight wiggle. The warmer the water use lighter colors and a wider wobble.

Fish into the wind, and fish all structure that will attract baitfish.

Do not go straight to a spinnerbait when you are fishing weeds; try a square billed bait and a lipless bait. The bass in the weeds see spinners, try a crankbait.

Learn to use crankbaits year-round. Using the right one for the correct situation will make you a much more successful bass fisherman.

Review

There is good information in this book that will make you fish better if you read it before you hit the water. I would be appreciative if you would go to the **Amazon site. And leave** a review so more people will read the book and we can spread the knowledge to everyone.

Here are a couple of blogs I update that contain tons of information on fishing bass.

Bass Fishing blog

Kayak fishing blog

Thanks again for reading my book.

Bass Fishing Tips Spinnerbaits

About this book

Thank you for checking out my book. The tips and information in this book will make you a better bass fisherman.

Remember that feeling when you caught your first fish? Bass fishing is special. If you are like me; you get that same feeling every time you catch a fish. It gets your adrenaline pumping. And there is something unique and special about that feeling.

Because we get that feeling, we want to experience it as often as possible. When you get time on the water, the main thing, you want to do is catch fish. This book is to help you spend more time catching fish and less time trying to find them.

When you fish for largemouth bass you will want to have a good selection of lures. You need spinner baits, crankbaits, jigs, and worms in your tackle box. There are so many variations of styles and colors, knowing which ones to pick can be overwhelming.

Spinner baits are one of the most versatile lures you can carry with you. They will catch fish in any water conditions, weather, and in every season of the year. Spinnerbaits along with crankbaits are the main water covering lures. They are the lures used to search out and find the active aggressive fish.

Anyone can catch bass on a spinnerbait or crankbait, by casting and reeling it back in. You do not want to spend most of your time on the water casting around the lake for a fish occasionally. You want to plan on a fish every cast.

The key is to plan to use your time in a way that you have the best chance to catch fish. If you have a plan, you will catch fish because you know where the fish should be. Also, because you know the best method of catching them on that day.

I will show you what types of spinnerbaits to use. Furthermore, show you where to use them and the best techniques to catch bass with spinnerbaits. This book is a good refresher to read before you head out on the lake. That way, you can spend most of your time catching fish instead of looking for them.

One key to success is to have a plan when you hit the lake

Here is a great book on how to fish a new lake.

Another informative book on How to fish crankbaits.

You will also like how to fish jigs.

And one more great read on how to fish plastic worms.

Having a plan will allow you to rule out 80% of the water in the lake before you even launch the boat. Following your plan is key. A plan will let you spend all your time fishing the other 20% of the lake where you know from your homework the fish will be.

Read through the book and use the tips throughout this book to help you spend more time catching fish. If you go at it with a plan, you will have confidence that you know where the fish will be. And what you can catch them on. You will be a much better fisherman.

Thank you for downloading my book. please **go to the Amazon site** and leave a review on the book, so more people will see the benefits.

If you have questions or comments, you can contact me at steve@stevepease.net Or visit **stevepease. net** for more great reads.

Table of Contents

Spinner Baits

One type of spinner bait

There are many things that affect how well the
Spinner bait will work on any specific day, or
even any hour. Two guys fishing in the same
boat with the identical lure can have different
levels of success.

I have been fishing many times where I would
start with a lure and cannot get anything to go
for it. I would go back to the same spot, later in
the day, and that lure was all they wanted.
Conditions change day to day, and sometimes
even more often. Be flexible. Because
something did not work earlier, does not mean
it will not work now.

The key is to find the right presentation. Give the bass something that will entice them into striking. Bass will strike because of hunger, or anger. It does not matter why, if they go after the bait.

There are several factors that can determine the amount of success you will have. Bass fishing is probably the hardest type of fishing there is because of all the options. Do they want a Jig? Do they want a crankbait? Do they want a worm? How about a grub or some other soft plastic lure? Is a spinnerbait the lure that will work? Then you must determine what type of spinnerbait the fish wants. You need to pick the spinner types, blade type, color, weight, and type of retrieve.

After all that, it can change within an hour, then you need to do it all over again. If you want to be the best bass fisherman you can be, you need to be proficient and confident fishing spinnerbaits. Spinnerbaits are the main search lure for active bass. Anyone can fish spinnerbaits. The key to being successful is to know where to throw it, how to retrieve it, and how to make it do what you want it to do.

The key to getting a spinnerbait to do what you want it to do is to fish it different from how most people do. Most fishermen throw the spinner bait out and bring it back to the boat with a steady retrieve. This technique will catch fish, sometimes a lot of fish. However, you can catch a lot more if you change a few things.

By changing little things in your retrieve, you can do things that will catch more bass. If you have ever watched a small fish in an aquarium or in the lake, you will see they do not swim in a straight line with no stops across the tank.

They will stop and start, and zig zag back and forth, and up and down. You want to imitate what small fish do; this is what the bass eats.

Spinner baits should always be one of your search lures. Search lures are the ones you use to find fish when you first fish for the day. You never know when you hit the water what the fish want for sure that day. You should have an idea, but you are never sure. The best way to start is to look for a pattern. What works this day? Keep track of what works. When you catch a fish, what color lure? What type of blade? what size lure? what retrieve were you using? How deep were you fishing? These things help you find the best pattern for the day.

Keeping track of these things will help you in the future. This can be valuable information next time you fish that lake. Here is a log that I use that you can access and use for tracking your fishing. You can print it and have a paper copy, or you can fill it out digitally.

If the fish are aggressive, you can catch them with a spinnerbait with a steady retrieve. If it is working, do not change it, keep catching them. Most lakes we fish in the northern U.S. that are natural lakes, we fish in a small area. Most of the fish will be in the areas withing 100 feet from the shore. Most lakes in Minnesota that we fish for bass, are 2000 acres or smaller. Even in the bigger lakes, the bass are in smaller areas.

Of those 2000 acres, there are only a couple of hundred acres where the Bass will be. Use spinnerbaits to find those aggressive bass. You can use them to cover the top spots quick, if you do not catch fish, go back over those spots with jigs and or worms, or crankbaits.

There are several things you need to think about when fishing spinner baits. Weather, wind, water temperature, food source, and time of year are important. What the bass are doing at the time you are fishing is also important. Are they spawning, post spawn, fattening for winter? These things are especially important to finding and catching bass.

As with other lures, working in and around cover will catch you more fish with spinnerbaits. Bass are ambush hunters. They need cover to ambush, and they need cover for their safety from larger predators. I keep stressing this because it is so important. ***Food source and cover are the keys to finding fish.***

My go to spinnerbait when I first get to the lake is a beetle spin. I have several styles and colors to pick from. I like the beetle spin because it can be fished very shallow, in thick weeds, around docks and lily pads. It is good on points and weed lines, and even in deeper water. The one above is one of my go to colors, pumpkin with green flakes.

The purple spinnerbait pictured above is one of my favorites. In the clear water lakes in

Minnesota, this color and type of bait have worked well for me. This bait and similar style baits are my choice when not using beetle spins. White with a double willow leaf blade is also good. An all-black bait with a silver Colorado blade is also effective. These are my three favorites.

Those 3 spinnerbaits are my go-to spinners for safety pin type baits. I have the most confidence in fishing them, so they work best for me. Confidence in fishing any bait is especially important in making sure you will be successful with it. If you want to fish a lure you need to have confidence in it. If not, you need to gain confidence from using it and getting comfortable with it. Focus on one bait for a period to gain confidence. A weekend, a week, or a month, whatever it takes.

Many years ago, when I was a new bass fisherman, I was confident with a spinnerbait, and a plastic worm, not so much with a jig. I would try it occasionally, but never enough to learn how to fish it. I decided to fish jigs only for a whole weekend.

I spent about 20 hours fishing only jigs. After a while, I felt more comfortable with them, and I caught fish. By the end of the weekend, I was greatly confident fishing and catching bass on jigs.

I found I like fishing jigs better with a spinning rod over a bait casting rod. I also found that jigs catch a lot of fish. I tried many jigs. I have found that I liked fishing a particular jig better than others. There are so many types now, I have added several other jigs to my arsenal. The point is fishing a type of lure until you know that you will catch fish with it.

One weekend gave me confidence to fish jigs. That confidence in fishing jigs has made me a better fisherman for many years. Do not get stuck in a rut where you only fish a single bait. It will not always be the best bait, and you will hurt your chances of catching the most bass you can. Be open-minded and try new things, but do not forget the baits you know work.

Why Spinnerbaits work

There are a few reasons that spinnerbaits work to catch fish. One reason is your bait is a threat to their nests or offspring. If you get your bait within the area that the fish is protecting, they will strike to keep the threat away. They are angry that this creature, your lure, is invading the area they have claimed as their territory. Predators do not like to share their space or their food.

Northern pike, like them or not, are a nice bonus to fishing spinnerbaits for bass. I catch a lot of pike while Bass fishing. They are fun to catch and are great to eat if you like to eat fish. I like to keep a Pike or two for a great dinner. If you want to learn the best way to clean them for eating, check out this video.

Pike are overly aggressive and good fighters. My brother and I were fishing one day, and he had a strike; it felt like a small Pike. He had it almost to the boat when it took off running straight down. He got it close to the boat where I could see it, and it was a big Pike, my guess it was in the 10 to 15-pound range.

When he got the fish within about 2 feet, the larger one let go. When he landed the smaller fish, it was only half a fish. Bitten in half by the larger one. The small fish was about a 13 or 14-inch fish. We call those hammer handles in Minnesota. Pike and their relatives the Muskie, will eat anything, even each other. Here is a short video of a muskie with a five- or six-pound pike in its mouth.

The third reason they work is because they are easy to fish, anyone can use a spinner bait and catch fish sometimes. All you must do to catch fish is to tie any spinner bait on your line and throw it out and reel it back in. Sometimes this works, and occasionally it works well.

To have spinnerbaits be the most effective for you; you need to have a variety of different blades, colors, size, style, and different retrieves.

Spinnerbaits will always be one of the top bass baits you can use. There is one big reason that spinnerbaits work for bass and for most fish. The spinner bait resembles the food that the bass loves to eat, smaller fish.

The way the spinnerbait moves, and the vibration put out by the spinnerbait looks like a bait fish. The flash from the blades of the spinner bait also attracts bigger fish. These things all add to the attraction that makes the Bass think it is something they want to eat.

When you are thinking about fishing baits. Or any fishing structure, or behavior, think about the food. What is the fish eating? Bass spend most of their time when the water is warmer looking for food because that is what they do. They eat when the water is warm to grow. They do not eat as much in colder water.

Getting the right combination of the bait looking like, and acting like, the main food for the Bass, will catch you more fish. Spinner baits are more effective because you can cover large areas of the lake fast. You can find the active and aggressive bass fast.

You can cover a house size area of water with a spinnerbait in 5 minutes. It would take you an hour to cover the same size area with a worm. The spinnerbait is a much faster way to attract active bass. After you catch the aggressive fish on spinnerbaits. Go back to the same areas and catch the not so aggressive fish on jigs and worms. You will have a great day fishing if you do this.

The key to having the best experience fishing is catching fish. If you are a tournament fisherman, or a weekend fisherman, you still want to catch the most fish you can. The way to do that is to get the extremely aggressive fish quick; that is where a spinnerbaits shine.

Types of spinnerbaits

Spinner baits come in five basic types.

- Inline
- Jig head with spinner
- Open safety pin type
- Buzz bait
- Live bait

The open safety pin type of spinner bait is by far the most common type used for Bass fishing, but the others are amazingly effective in certain situations and for some fish.

The Inline spinnerbait

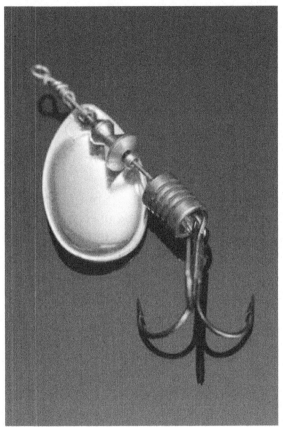

This is a typical in line spinner bait.

I will go over the inline and live bait rigs because they are useful. But this book is about safety pin type, the jig head type and buzz baits for largemouth bass in natural northern lakes.

There are many variations of in line spinnerbaits. They all work the same and other than color and material, they look similar. They come in different colors. Different sizes and with multiple blades, and different skirts. Mepps and Rooster tail are the most well-known manufacturers. There are other makers of in line spinner baits, but these are the biggest.

In line spinner baits are not often used for largemouth Bass in natural lakes. Because they are not weedless. The exposed treble hooks will catch most any weed near them. Most fishing in natural lakes for largemouth bass happens in and around weeds. Also, around other structure that will catch your spinnerbait hooks. There is one exception. They are highly effective on schooling largemouth bass in deeper water on reservoirs.

I have used and had good success within line spinners in the BWCA in northern Minnesota. They work well for fishing for smallmouth bass. In those lakes there are few weeds, and the smallmouth are holding to rocky structure.

In line spinner baits are also highly effective in river fishing. But you must be careful if you do not want to lose many of them. They are great at hooking rocks and branches, common in most rivers.

In line baits will catch most types of fish. If you have a place where you can fish it without getting snagged a lot, do not be afraid to use them. The fish seldom miss inline baits, like they do with other types of spinnerbaits.

When I was a kid growing up in Northwestern Pennsylvania. I spent hours fishing in rivers. I mostly fished with in line spinnerbaits. Most of the fish I caught were smallmouth bass and pike. They do work in areas that do not have lots of weeds. My favorites were a black and yellow mepps, and a yellow rooster tail with black spots and a yellow hair tail.

One other place I have caught fish on in line spinners it to reel them fast over the tops of weeds. Kind of like an inline buzz bait, but lower in the water, and smaller.

Live bait rigs

Live bait rigs are common in Minnesota and surrounding states. One of the most used and popular rigs is the Lindy rig. That is a staple for Walleye fisherman.

In the right situations, and if you use live bait for bass, you can catch them on live bait rigs. My wife caught 3 bass this past summer over 5 pounds and many other nice bass. Fishing from the dock with a sucker minnow on a bobber rig. Bass like real injured fish and artificial.

Jig head with spinner blade

This bait may not appear at first look a bait you would care to use. Do not be too quick to pass this bait over. The bait I am talking about is a Beetle spin bait, made by the Johnsons lure company. This bait comes in many sizes and colors. It is adaptable to many different situations.

They have added a new version that has a living rubber skirt instead of a grub. The live rubber skirted ones work well also. They are amazingly effective and easy to fish.

Another great thing about the beetle spin is that you can catch anything with this bait. If I could have only one bait to fish with anywhere for any fish, I would pick the beetle spin, because it is so versatile. You can take off the spinner blade, and it makes a great jig. You can put any color or style of grub trailer on it, and it goes through weeds.

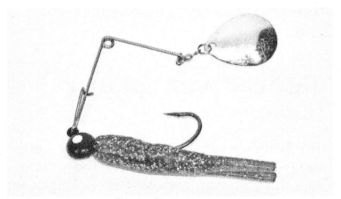

Johnson Beetle Spin

This one is a saltwater version. I buy these because they are bigger, ½ oz., than the freshwater versions, more bulk, more flash, more vibration. It works well as a flutter bait when fishing docks and points.

I have also used Beetle spins with a rubber skirt made for safety pin type spinnerbaits. Put a rubber leg skirt on it, add a trailer. Anything you want to do with it. Take off the spinner and use it as a jig. It is the most versatile bait there is. They also are remarkably effective for many types of fish.

The road runner is another version that also can work well. The spinner is under the jig head and is great for bumping off structure and getting attention.

The roadrunner lure is another good bass lure that is a Crappie lure. But in the spring and other times when the bass want them, they are great baits. Because of the head shape and the hook up high, they work around trees and rocks.

You can add size and bulk to roadrunners by changing the grub to a 4 inch. They are also good on flats where there are light weeds, and good on points and drop offs, much like a jig with flash. Roadrunners are also good for rivers and for boundary waters lakes.

Open safety pin type

By far the most popular style, because they work. There are a few different styles; there are short arm, long arm, twisted wire, and open wire options. I do not like the untwisted wire style; they say they are stronger and easier to make. They may be less expensive to make. And they may be stronger. However, I have never had a twisted wire break on a fish, and I have caught many good size Pike on the twisted ones.

They also say the open ones are easier to keep running straight. That may be, but I find they foul way more often when casting, and that ruins your chances of catching a fish on that cast. You must reel it in and fix it and throw it back out.

The purple spinner bait at the beginning is a twisted wire; the one below is an open wire style. The place where you tie up is a twist in the wire; the line stays there and cannot slide up the wire to the jig head and foul up the bait. The one below is an open style. I use them because they are more common, but I do not use them if I do not need to. I always use a leader with a swivel when fishing spinner baits.

Because of where I fish, I always catch Pike and Bass. Pike have razor-sharp teeth that will cut your line. I do not want to lose a good Pike or an expensive spinner bait because of no leader, and I do not feel they catch fewer fish. I do not think the bass can see that extra piece of wire on the bait. They are looking at the flash of the blades.

I also do not think the fish would survive with a spinnerbait stuck in its mouth, and I do not want to kill any fish I will not eat.

The snap slides away from where it should stay when you cast. It fouls up the spinner bait, and you lose a potential fish catching cast because you must fix it.

For bass fishing, I use ¼ oz., ½ oz., and ¾ oz. spinner baits, depending on where I am fishing, and the water temp. Colder water use smaller baits and retrieve slower.

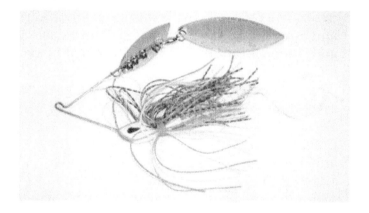

Types of blades

There are 3 basic types of spinner blades.

- Colorado
- Indiana
- Willow leaf blade

The previous picture spinner bait has a double willow leaf blade. The roadrunner lure above is an Indiana blade. And the grape-colored spinner at the beginning is a Colorado blade.

The main difference between the three of them. The Colorado blade has more vibration and more flash. The Indiana blade has flash and some vibration. And the willow leaf blade has lots of flash and some vibration. A combination willow leaf and Colorado give the most flash and the most vibration.

Colorado blades are better for helicoptering and a yoyo retrieve. Because the bait falls slower and has lots of flash and vibration. A willow leaf blade is better in weeds. The blades pull through weeds easier and gives lots of fish attracting flash.

Buzz baits

Buzz baits are top water baits and spinnerbaits. They are highly effective at certain times and are a blast to fish.

There are a few different buzz baits. There are inline ones like a regular inline spinnerbait. You retrieve them on the surface. There are the ones like safety pin type spinnerbaits. They have two or three plastic or metal blades above the body.

I use both types, but I prefer the inline ones, because for me, they hook more strikes. Topwater buzz baits attract a lot of fish, but the fish miss, sometimes they miss a lot. The inline one I use most has a hair body and a weed guard, so I can drag it across thick weeds with little trouble.

I have caught both Bass and Pike on this lure and many of them. There are not a lot of choices for inline buzz baits. And the ones you can find are expensive, but you should have one at least. The trailer hooks help catch more strikes. It is not uncommon for the bass to miss topwater baits. Use a trailer hook if you can.

In line buzz bait

Overhead buzz bait

A Rebel buzz'N Frog is another in line buzz bait I have success with. It is strange looking, but it works, and has caught me some fish.

Adding a trailer hook to your buzz baits is a key to getting more of the short strikes, so you can land a lot more fish. The three bladed black one above you can fish slower because of the extra lift from the three blades.

A tip many fishermen use when fishing buzz baits is not to look at them when you are retrieving them. That way you will not set the hook until you feel it and jerk it out of the fish's mouth. It is hard not to watch a buzz bait, but you do not want to set it too early. There are even strikes you can see coming from a long way away.

If you are getting a lot of short strikes, and you are using a trailer hook. Try not watching as you retrieve the bait, you may react too fast and jerk it out of the mouth of the fish.

Vary your retrieve when fishing buzz baits, faster or slower. I have seen where I can reel it as quick as I can crank it, and they go for it. And sometimes just reeling it fast enough to keep it on the surface works. Buzz baits are great search baits; do not forget about them when you get on the water.

Some fishermen also use a trick of tuning the buzz bait by bending the wire to the side. This makes it run to the right or left on purpose. When fishing next to structure like a dock or a wall, you can make the bait go under the dock and crash into posts and walls.

Another trick is if you are getting short strikes. Have a straight worm ready on another rod and throw it at the same spot where the strike was.

Buzz baits can work from 60 degrees in the spring, all the way to 50 degrees in the fall. It may not work every day, but you should always have one ready.

Where to fish Spinnerbaits

You can fish spinnerbaits everywhere and catch fish. Certain types work better at times under different conditions. So, what are the choices you can make that will help you catch more fish?

Docks

Docks are not the prime spots for spinnerbaits if the fish are not aggressive. Jigs and worms are better dock baits when they are holding tight to the structure. If the fish are active, you can find them with a spinnerbait on docks.

When casting to docks, one key is to use a low trajectory type of cast, that will allow the spinner bait to hit the water with a small splash and a quiet entry into the water. Learn a low forehand and a low backhand cast to get you to the right spot without spooking the fish.

The more isolated a dock is, the more likely it will hold bigger bass.

Docks that have the deck closer to water level also hold more bass. They are harder to cast under, but they are better because there is more shade, and the fish feel more protected.

Wooden post docks are better than metal post docks. Fish them all, but never pass up a wooden leg dock. There are few wooden leg docks in the northern lakes. The water freezes, and the docks must come out before it freezes over. Every year we put in the dock in spring and take it out in fall. This makes it much easier to have steel or aluminum posts for docks.

Docks on points are good, docks with steep shorelines are also productive, and docks with rocky shorelines are hotspots for bass. Look for docks that are in the shade, or have brush piles near them, or other cover nearby. If there are lily pads or weed beds near the dock that makes it more attractive to bass as well.

Make sure you cover each edge and hit the posts if you can as you retrieve the bait back to the boat.

A Beetle spin spinnerbait, and a road runner are good dock lures. You can throw them up under the dock easier, you can skip them, and you can shoot them under the dock. This is a technique for crappie fishing in southern lakes. But it has worked well for me on Bass with a roadrunner spinner on northern lakes. Try this technique on your favorite lake.

Weeds

Fishing weeds with spinnerbait is a place they shine. You can cover lots of water fast and pick up the active aggressive Bass. If there is structure in the weeds, fish it. Weeds are good structure in themselves. The weeds create pockets and places for Bass to wait and ambush food. Not all weeds are good for fish. Some are much better than others.

There is a lake I fish that has a huge flat about 6 feet deep that is a giant bed of cabbage weed. The best way to fish this bed is to go upwind and drift over it. I have done this so many times and have caught hundreds of fish, largemouth Bass, smallmouth Bass and Pike. They all love cabbage weed and will sit anywhere in it. Never pass up a bed of cabbage weed.

When fishing the cabbage weed flats with spinnerbaits, I use the double willow leaf bladed bait. I fancast from the edges into and through the weeds, the willow leaf blade comes through the weeds with fewer hang ups. The flash will draw the bass from a good distance. Even a good size Colorado blade will come through the cabbage weed. Use a Colorado blade if you need more vibration to get them to strike.

I have had days when I have caught over 30 bass and Pike from the weed flats. When they are in the weed flats, they have almost no time see what the flash is. They will attack the spinner with ferocity. Bass and Pike are not shy.

I have personal and up-close experience with them. I raised two largemouth bass and a Pike in an aquarium a few years back and watched them grow. I watched how they feed. I fed them fathead minnows twice a week. They grew fast. It was so cool to watch them swim up to the minnows, flared their gills, and the minnows disappeared by the bass sucking them in.

The pike was different. He would sometimes even get a mouth full of gravel from the bottom of the tank, his attacks were vicious.

The two bass grew from 4-inch size to close to 3 pounds in a year. The Pike grew from about 6 inches to 20 inches at the same time. I learned a lot about Bass and Pike, and about how they feed. It was only a 100-gallon aquarium, so I could not test lures on them, but I watched and learned a lot. Follow the food and you will find the fish.

I would add structure of different types to the aquarium to see how they would react. They would take up a spot near the structure. The pike seemed less drawn by the structure than the bass.

Points

Fishing points with spinnerbaits works best by positioning your boat on the windy side of the point. Cast toward shore, pull the spinner through the weeds near the shore, if there are weeds. When the bait gets through the weeds, let it flutter down to the bottom.

I like to use a short arm spinnerbait like the one below. The short arm baits flutter better and will draw strikes on the fall. They can also work slower, which works good fishing down a gradual drop off.

If it hits the bottom, and you have not gotten a strike. Raise up the rod tip and crank it twice and then let it flutter back down. Work the bait down the slope of the point.

Another option is to park the boat on the windy side of the point and cast into the weeds near the shore. Then cast across the front of the weeds where the Bass will sit to ambush the bait fish. After you cover that side, move to the other side of the point.

After fishing both sides, move on to the next piece of structure you will fish, or go over the same areas with a jig or a worm.

Drop offs

I see people all the time moving along the shoreline, casting toward the shore. Then they crank their spinner bait back to the boat with a steady retrieve. You can catch fish that way. However, you will catch many more if you vary your retrieve. When you get your bait to the edge of the weeds, let it drop and do a yoyo retrieve back to the boat. Or at least do a ripping motion every few cranks.

Bass are looking up most of the time. They will travel up quite a way to get something they want to eat. However, if you are way above them retrieving the bait at a steady fast retrieve, they will most likely not come that far up. Or it is way past them before they can react. Getting down closer to where they are, will get you more bites.

Seasonal

There are some seasonal differences that will affect your spinnerbaits. In the northern part of the country, at least in Minnesota and Wisconsin. We have seasons for Bass that close until mid-May in Wisconsin and the end of May in Minnesota.

We do not have spring Bass fishing in Minnesota, although sometimes the end of May is still spring like. We are past spawn when the season opens, so we are in the transition period with the water temp around 60 degrees.

The main thing to remember in the spring is to use baits that are smaller. And slow down your fishing presentation. If you are like me, you want to cover a lot of water and keep moving. However, it will pay off to slow down and let them have more time to go for your bait when they are not as aggressive.

In the summer when the water temps get in the upper 60s and above. You can fish the bigger, noisier baits, and fish them faster. Still do not forget the ripping motion, or something different. You are trying to make the bait look like an injured baitfish.

They will go after baitfish that are healthy. However, if they think it is injured. It is an easier catch, and they will go for it fast. If you have ever watched baitfish, you notice they do not swim straight through an area fast. They stop and start and dart side to side. If you can imitate that movement and look injured, your bait will be a meal.

Kevin Van Dam, one of the top pro bass fishermen says. "Almost all fisherman fish too fast, and you will improve your catches if you slow down year-round." He fishes a slower retrieve with a ripping motion most of the time.

In the fall, keep at it. If you stop fishing after Labor Day, you are missing out on the best time of year to catch your largest Bass. The big Bass get aggressive and want to eat all they can in the fall. They know their metabolism is slowing down and they need to get fat before they do not want to eat much. Do not miss out on this great time for fishing.

Winter in Minnesota is not for Bass fishing. People catch Bass through the ice sometimes, but I am not one to sit on a frozen lake in a spot and fish. Casting is my thing, and I like to move and search out the fish and not wait for them to come, besides, it is cold.

Tying it all together

When you are looking for active Bass in colder water with spinnerbaits, a favorite lure is a smaller beetle spin with a 3-inch curly tail grub. Use a Colorado blade so you can fish it slower.

Spinner baits are the number-one bait for tournament fishermen in the spring. You need to use them in the spring to fish at your best.

In clear water, use white or colors that look like baitfish. White with other colors in the skirts will work well. In dark or stained water use natural colors with orange added or chartreuse. The blue looks like a bluegill. Orange gives the look of crawfish, and the fire tiger-colored baits look like sunfish.

Learn to cast underhand or sidearm. This will allow you to land the bait with as little splash and commotion as possible. A big splash on the water above the fish will not be good to attract them.

Retrieves

There are several types of retrieves. First is cranking it back to the boat. This is not the best to use most of the time, although this is the retrieve that many fishermen use almost all the time.

Slow rolling Works great for fishing deep and in cold water. You want to keep the bait moving all the time, but at a slow crank. Crank it only fast enough to keep the blade turning. You also want to keep it hitting the bottom, or whatever structure is under your bait.

Ripping—this is Kevin Van Dam's favorite retrieve. The way you do this is to use a regular retrieve. However, every 3 or four cranks, rip the bait toward you, then start the retrieve again.

Stop start—I use this retrieve or the ripping most of the time. With this retrieve you crank a couple of times, with or without an up down jerk, then stop for a second or two, and repeat.

Walking the bait—retrieve the spinner fast enough to make the blade bulge the surface of the water. This works well over flooded timber or weeds right below the surface.

Jigging—This technique is the one to use on points and drop-offs and around structure.

Dragging—this is the same way you fish a worm, dragging it on the bottom. This is a great technique for big Bass.

Yo-yo—this retrieve is like a slow roll, except it is faster. You reel slow and lift the rod tip and let it flutter back down every few cranks.

These are the most effective retrieves. The key is to always do something on your retrieve to make the bait look like an injured bait fish.

The steady retrieve will work best only a small percentage of the time. Work every cast by making it do something different. Being different will make your bait look better than most other fisherman's lures. The variations will make it look injured. Think about what a baitfish would do, it will not swim at a steady speed in a straight line.

On points

Fan cast from the windy side of the point up into the weeds. Let the spinnerbait fall when it gets past the weed line. Let it flutter down to the bottom and yoyo or use the start stop retrieve to bring the bait back to the boat.

Use these tips and techniques when fishing spinner baits. You will catch more bass and you will be a better fisherman.

If you think this book will help you be a better fisherman. I would appreciate if you would go to Amazon and write a review about this book

Thank you again for reading my book. Now go catch lots of fish.

Bass Fishing Tips

How to fish Jigs

Introduction

Denny Brauer, a former FLW angler of the
year said, many anglers get hung up on
versatility. Brauer said. "You need to be
versatile, but you also need to master the key
techniques to be a great bass fisherman. For
me that is jig fishing. When conditions are
right for jigs, my chances for winning
tournaments improve dramatically."

The important thing to take from this quote is:
One of the top pro bass fishermen of all times
loves jigs. He says jig fishing improves his
chances of winning a tournament. Being a
great jig fisherman, will improve your fish
catches as well.

I will go over the best tips for fishing bass with
jigs. We will cover all aspects of jig fishing. We
will go over seasonal changes, color, where to
fish, and how to fish. When you finish the
book, you will have the tools to be the best jig
fisherman you can be.

Why should you use jigs? General knowledge
among bass fisherman is jigs will not always
catch more bass. However, they will catch
bigger bass most of the time.

One thing you do not want to do for bass
fishing is to be a jack of all trades, and a

master of none. The best option is to be proficient with all bass lures. Spinner baits, crankbaits, top water baits, worms, and jigs. This takes work and time.

You want to be able to catch bass under all conditions and situations. This takes time and you need to do it in stages, so you are not a master of none of the bass techniques.

Being an expert with several baits is an important part of being a great bass fisherman. To get there, you will have to work on it. If you can only be great with a couple of baits, learn to fish a spinnerbait first, then learn to fish a jig well.

The spinnerbait is your search lure to find aggressive fish. The jig is the second most versatile lure, because you can fish it many ways. Swim jigs can be used as a search lure as well. You can pitch it, flip it, fish it like a worm, even put a spinner on it, and it is a spinnerbait.

You can fish jigs year-round and catch bass. You can catch more fish with worms than jigs, but if you are looking for bigger bass, the jig is the way to go. That is why many pros will choose a jig. The pros are going for weight, so bigger is always better. Worm fishing is important to learn as well. It takes more patience, but it is a great technique that will catch a lot of bass and you should learn it.

The reason that jigs work so well on bass is because bass love to eat crayfish. Crayfish are their food of choice where they are available, and jigs look like crayfish to bass.

You can fish jigs in areas with cover as with most bass lures. You can also fish jigs in the cover that you cannot fish any other type of lure. Learn how to take full advantage of bass cover, and the way they ambush their food. This will make you a better jig fisherman and a great bass fisherman. You can fish jigs almost anywhere and, in any conditions, and catch bass.

Most fish most of the time are lazy and do not want to work any harder than they need to for their food. That is one reason live bait works great for catching bass.

My wife caught these two bass within a couple of minutes from our dock last year.

Make the bait look injured. Make it look like an easy meal, make it look like what the fish are eating, and most of the time, you will catch them.

I wrote this book, like my other fishing books, so you can read them before you head out to the lake. You will have the tips and ideas fresh in your mind. Then when the need arises to try something different, you have it right there, ready to use.

This was a great catch. It was my birthday. I had gotten a new rod and reel and some brand-new jigs. We got to the lake, I walked down to the water and tossed out the Nutech jig in the picture below. About halfway back working the jig I felt the jig stop so I set the hook. It was the first cast of the season with all new equipment. A six-pound bass, what a great catch.

Table of Contents

Tackle

Opinions vary between bass fisherman about what equipment to use for jig fishing. My choice for jig and worm fishing is a 7'2" Shimano jig and worm rod, medium heavy with a fast tip.

I like this rod because it has enough backbone to pull the bass out of the thick stuff. It also has a sensitive enough tip so you can feel what is going on at the other end of the line.

For a reel, I like Shimano spinning reels. They have been my favorites since they started making them. I love the quick-fire reels because I love the quickfire trigger. I love the ability of one-handed casting with spinning gear. Once you use it for a while; it is so quick and easy.

I also prefer to fish jigs and worms on spinning gear instead of baitcasting gear, I like the feel of the lure better. The exception is swim jigs. I prefer to fish the faster baits, swim jigs, spinners, and crankbaits on baitcasting gear.

I carry four rods with me, so I am ready, three baitcasting, one with a spinner tied on and one with a crankbait tied on, and one with a Silver minnow or swim jig. The other one is the spinning rod with a worm or a jig.

As far as line goes. I use fluorocarbon on my spinning rig most of the time. The fluorocarbon does not have the memory coiling that happens with mono. I use braid on all my baitcasters. I like braid for the strength and for the thinner size, and no memory in the line. The strength of the braid is amazing.

My wife caught a rock in the river, I wrapped the line around my arm, with my jacket on and started walking until it came loose. I straightened out the hook. The line did not break.

The tackle you choose is more about what you like and what you feel comfortable with. There is nothing wrong with good quality monofilament line. I used trilene xt for 30 years and never had a problem with it. Your choice of rods, reels, and line has less to do with catching fish. Knowledge and confidence are much more important. If you like a set up, and you feel more comfortable fishing it, that will help you catch more bass.

Jig Color

For jig color, there is a lot of discussion about what colors are better, or if it even matters at all. Some fishermen do not think color makes much difference. Some think it makes a big difference. The ability to see color in water changes a lot as you go deeper, depending on the colors.

Color makes a difference. However, size and presentation, and if it looks like the bass choice of food are more important than color.

There are hundreds of colors and color combinations you can pick from. It is not as bad as going to pick out paint colors, but close. There are some that seem to be better than others. The key is not to choose colors you think look cool. It is easy to fall for that trap.

Many lure manufacturers make lures to attract fisherman and fish. You do not need every possible color of the spectrum. I am guilty of getting sucked into what looks cool. I have several lures that appeal to me by looks, not necessarily what the fish want.

There have been a few unofficial, unscientific studies done. They are asking fishermen to tell them what the best color they have found for jigs.

The top colors submitted are.
- Black Blue
- Black, blue flash
- Black, brown crawfish
- Olive pumpkin
- Green pumpkin
- Brown purple
- PBJ flash
- Peanut Butter Jelly

There are more color combinations that catch Bass. Many have caught Bass for thousands of anglers. These seem to have been the best color combinations for many years.

Most fishermen know bass love skirted jigs. There are now many types of skirt material. I like the newer silicone or live rubber ones. The reason Jigs work so well is because jigs look like crayfish. Crayfish are a preferred food source for bass in lakes from north to south.

I have found from experience that the above colors cover most of what I have had success with. Everyone has used black and blue with success. One of my other favorites is a brown, orange skirt, looks like the food, looks like a crawfish.

It depends a lot on what the forage fish is in that body of water. I would recommend starting with black and blue or black and brown. After that I would try a brown and orange, or a mix of green and black or green and brown.

These are general guidelines that seem to produce well.

- Shallow and dark water. The best colors seem to be combinations of black and blues. Black and reds, June bug and other bluegill colored, darker colored skirts.
- Deeper clear water impoundments. The browns and brown purple and the PBJ combinations seem to produce best.
- In areas of shallow clearer weedier water. The greens, and green pumpkin, and olive watermelon combinations seem to produce best.

Here is another general pattern. Largemouth go more for the black based colors. While Smallmouth bass go more for the brown based colors.

My favorite colors for largemouth are the brown, orange color, and the black and blue colors. I prefer green pumpkin and the PB and J in shallow weedy clear water. Keep an open mind on color, when nothing is working, try something different. It may be the trigger to turn them on.

General Tips

Denny Brauer said about jigs. "It is the most versatile bait in fishing." Brauer also says, "One of the main reasons I use jigs is because I like to catch big fish. I don't know of any other bait out there that appeals more to quality fish than a jig does."

He said, "jigs penetrate the heavy cover better than other lures. "They also hook and hold a higher percentage of fish."

There are a thousand different jigs you can get. They vary in size, weight, head shape, color, skirt type, skirt size, hook style. They also can have a weed guard or no weed guard, long skirts, short skirts, trailer, or no trailer, etc.

Here are general tips to remember when jig fishing.

- Jig fishing needs concentration: you must pay attention to what is going on below the surface.
- Fish jigs slow most of the time, slower when water is cold.
- Largemouth Bass prefer larger jigs than smallmouth bass.
- Jigs are great night fishing lures.

The most important thing to consider in jigs is the size. The size is critical to catching the most fish. If you want to catch bigger fish, stay with the bigger jigs, if you want to catch more fish, drop a size.

This is a general rule. I have caught some huge bass on small jigs, but the normal is bigger jig, bigger bass. Trailers count as to the size. If you add a big trailer, you have a bigger jig.

You want the jig to be heavy enough to get the jig down to where you want it in the water, but not heavier than what it needs to be. Like a worm, the slow dropping bait will attract more fish than a heavy jig sinking to the bottom like a rock.

I have caught most of my bass on jigs in the 1/4 and 3/8 oz. size. In the northern lakes of Minnesota and Wisconsin where I do most of my fishing, these sizes have been the best for me. Unless your Flippin into thick weeds, I would not go bigger than 3/8 most times. If you want a bigger jig, add a bigger plastic trailer to the jig or a bigger skirt.

Here are the recommended weights of jigs for specific types of fish.

Panfish and Crappies 1/32, 1/16, 1/8 oz.
Trout and Salmon 1/16, 1/8, 1/4 oz.
Walleyes and Bass 1/16, 1/8, 1/4, 3/8, 1/2 oz.

Northern Pike and Muskies 3/4, 1, 1 ¼, 1 1/2 oz.
Lake Trout and Stripers ¾, 1, 1 ½, 2 oz.

For big bass and situations where weeds are thick, ¾ and 1 oz jigs or even bigger for bass are not uncommon.

How to fish Jigs

A jig is most of the time a drop bait. You cast the jig to the spot, engage the reel or not, and let it drop to the bottom on a tight line or on a slackline. Let it sit for a minute or longer, then take up the slack and jiggle it around once or twice.

If the jig is not hit, move the jig up and toward you. Then let it drop back to the bottom. Repeat the wait and jiggle, repeat it over again a couple more times. If no takers bring it back and try a different spot.

Many strikes will come on the initial drop. It may only feel like a stop, or a slight twitch; you may feel it move away. If you feel any of these things, take up the slack and use a sweeping motion to set the hook.

One key with jigs. Like with most lures in shallow water, is you want the jig to enter the water with as little noise as possible. Learn how to cast with the jig close to the water. You want it to hit so it comes in with as little splash and noise as you can. This is important in not scaring the fish away.

Learn what the jig feels like when it is lying on the bottom, think about what it is doing. When you feel something different than when it is lying there alone, set the hook. Many bass hits are a tap or a slight move. They do not hit it like a fast-moving lure, most hits are very subtle.

If you have a weed guard on the jig, set it more like you would a Texas rigged worm. Set it harder to draw the hook past the weed guard and into the fish's mouth.

Do not be afraid to let the jig sit still for longer than you may think. Then shake it once or twice without moving it toward you. Do not be afraid to set the hook hard.

Seasonal

Spring

In the spring, you want to go with slow falling lighter jigs. The bass are sluggish and not moving fast because of the cold water. I like to use an 1/8 or ¼ oz. jig with a grub trailer.

One of my all-time favorites in colder water is a Roadrunner jig. It has a grub trailer with a small spinner on the bottom side. They work well for bass in colder water.

A jig with a crayfish trailer is also good in colder water. You should cast and let the jig drop to the bottom. Then reel up the slack and give it a twitch to make it shake like a dying fish.

As the water warms up, you can move the jig faster and even hop it along the bottom.

When fishing docks in cold water, let it sit after the cast for up to a minute or even longer. You will startle the fish if a jig drops into the water. If the jig lands a couple of inches away from the fish, you need to give them time to come and investigate. Once their initial shock from the lure landing goes away, they will check it out.

Bass will move into the shallows in the spring. When they do this, points and drop offs are one of the key places to find them with slow fished jigs. Look for points and drop offs with any weeds, this is the first cover they will go to as the weeds grow.

In cold water, a drag and shake retrieve works well. Let the jig drop to the bottom, let it sit, drag it a few inches and give it a shake, then let it sit again, and repeat.

Summer

In the summer, jigs are great for fishing docks and other structure and thicker weeds. You can use bigger jigs in the summer. Because the bait fish they eat are larger, that is what they are looking for, so go bigger with your baits.

Jigs are great dock baits year-round. I like to come up to a dock and fish across the front, hop the jig along the front of the dock. Then move to where you can cast down one side and hop it out, next fish down the other side and hop it back.

If the dock is a big dock, throw the jig up under the dock. Most of the docks in the northern states are only 4 feet wide, because they cannot survive ice. They must come out in the fall and be put back in the spring.

If you are fishing heavy weeds, you need to pick a jig that is big enough to get through the mat of weeds. Once through the top it can then get to the bottom. Go with the lightest jig you can, that will get through the weed matt.

Once the jig goes through the mat, let it drop straight to the bottom. If it does not get hit, give it a little hop, if still no hit, pull it out and try a different spot.

This is a Flippin technique; you find the holes and drop the jig in the holes, then go on to the next hole.

Fall and winter

As the water temp drops, jigs still work well. You need to change your technique. You need to fish slower. Focus on shorelines with steep drop-offs and deeper coves. Furthermore, look for long points that drop off into deeper water.

Look for flooded trees and any remaining weeds; make sure you fish any docks that are still in the water.

Look for areas that have warmer water. If you can find an area that is 5 to 10 degrees warmer, it can make a huge difference.

Start with the lightest possible jig for the conditions. You want to feel what the jig is doing; a good starting point is ¼ to 3/8 oz.

Head Styles

There are tons of jig heads and variations of jig head styles. I will not attempt to list them all. This is a short breakdown of the ones I use and have found to be the most effective jigs for catching bass.

There are many different head styles for jigs. The variety of shapes and styles do different things for different situations. Jig head shapes are oval, round, football, stand up, skipping head, swim jigs heads, and many slight variations of those. There are variations of these that are different, but they are like these shapes.

Many bass jigs also have a weed guard, that help you fish in heavy cover and get fewer snags.

The football head jigs are one of the best to use on rocky bottoms without getting hung up. Bullet or oval or longer head jigs work best in weedy areas. The heads slide through the weeds best because they have no corners to get hung up.

Arky style jig heads are one of my favorites. They are great for Flippin into heavy weeds. Also dragging through wood and other structure. Football jigs work best in rocks and Arky heads will work best almost everywhere else. I would classify it as a long oval style head, and it also stands up well.

Another big jig for me in heavy cover is the Booyah Boo Jig. They come in lots of good colors, and have a heavy weed guard and a nice, shaped head for pulling through weeds.

Nutech jigs are one of my new favorites. The jig at the beginning that I caught that nice fish on is a Nu tech jig. These are a great stand-up jig. They are a type of football jig. Basically, I use two main types of jigs, a stand up for a slow presentation, and a swim jig type head for quicker presentation where more weeds are involved.

Another one of my favorite jigs is the Roadrunner jig. They have a small spinner on the underside of the jig. They also have an unusual head shape that makes them snag resistant.

They are a great Crappie jig, but in the bigger models with a nice curly tail trailer on them, they are a killer bass lure. I have had great results fishing docks with roadrunner jigs.

The bigger ones are not as easy to find. But Bass Pro carries the ¼ oz size, and so does Cabela's, or you can get them from Blakemore.

Skirts

Most skirts are live rubber or silicone. Some have newer types of plastic. There are still skirts made from animal hair and types of marabou. They come in many colors, solids, and patterns.

The various skirt materials will make the jig look different. When the jig is sitting still or moving. Some fishermen think they look more lifelike than others. It is a subtle difference, and under tough conditions, it may change the way it works.

Matching the colors to the baitfish the bass are eating in the lake is still the key to getting the most bites. Adding a trailer can give you an advantage. Adding the extra bulk to the jig and adding a variation in color and attraction can also work.

Use a trailer that enhances or matches the jig color. You can use pork or plastic; pork will dry out, so they are not used often anymore. The soft plastic is much easier to use. Plastic can last for a long time, and not get hard like pork.

It is not a skirt, but it is effective under some conditions. I am talking about hair jigs. They are not used much for Bass fishing, but they can be fantastic in cold water that is clear.

Again, you want to match the jig to look like the forage the Bass are eating, and you want to fish them slow. For hair jigs, you also want to use small jigs, up to 3/8 oz.

The best colors are:

- **Black** -- Looks like a leach
- **Brown** -- Looks like a crawfish
- **White** -- Looks like minnows or shad
- **Chartreuse** -- Looks like perch, or sunfish.
- **Smoke Gray** -- Looks like most minnows.

The way to fish these jigs is to drag them along the bottom, do not hop or bounce them, drag them in the mud or sand. The jig is to imitate larva and small baby creatures.

Places to fish Jigs

Weeds

In many articles, you will read people saying they use certain lures when fishing grass. They mean weeds not just grass only. Jigs can be great to fish in all kinds of weeds, from thick Hydrilla to sparse scattered weeds.

They are the only lure you can use for the super thick stuff. Dropping the jig into holes in the weeds can catch lots of Bass. It is called Flippin.

If the vegetation is not as heavy, you can use swim jigs to fish over the top of and through the weeds.

When you fish in deeper weed beds, fish the jig on points or v's in the weed beds and outside edges. Bass focus on edges so they can ambush their prey easier. Hit the outside edges first. Then look for the inside edges that have something different.

Any other structure in the weeds can also be a perfect spot. A log or post or a dock are all prime locations. Even the shade from an overhanging tree or a boat can be a structure to the fish. Because it has defined edges and offers shade, the bass will relate to it.

If you are fishing a river or anywhere there is current. Look for something blocking the flow. A log or a rock rip rap. Then look for the Bass to sit on the back side of the object facing the current flow waiting for food to come to them.

Deep Water

If you are fishing deep water structure with a jig, use a medium size jig. Fish with a swimming retrieve, with a bouncing motion by pumping the rod tip up and down and pause occasionally. Cast the jig past the spot and let it sink to the desired depth. Once it is on the bottom, use the swimming retrieve through the structure.

Docks

I always fish docks with jigs. It is the best lure there is for covering all the prime places under and around a dock. I fish spinnerbaits and crankbaits and worms around docks as well. But my first choice is a swim jig, then a bottom finesse jig.

My favorite colder water dock jig is a black or a white roadrunner jig. Work it along the front first, then along both sides. Then if you can, get it under the dock and hit the dock posts when retrieving the jig. As the water warms up, go to a bigger swim jig. I like a white swim jig with a white twin tail trailer. Fish it like a spinnerbait just under the surface. Fish across the front and down each side. then go under if you can.

When you go to the finesse jig, try the sit, and wait technique first, then try fishing with a pumping motion. If no bites, try hopping it along the bottom. Often, the slower presentation will work better and catch more fish.

Shooting docks is a cool technique I discovered a couple years ago from a YouTube video. It is a crappie technique that will catch lots of bass. It is cool and lets you get under the docks. Works best on wide docks. Check out this video and see the technique. Let me know if you have tried it, it is amazingly effective for getting under docks. This technique also lets the lure hit the surface quietly and with little splash.

When you are fishing the deeper front side of the dock, cast past and retrieve it up to the dock. Then work it past the dock. When you are fishing the sides and throwing into the shallow water, let the jig sit. Let it sit after the cast on the bottom for up to a minute or two before you start your retrieve.

When the jig hits in a few inches of water, letting the fish get over the initial scare will help you catch a lot more Bass. If you find a dock with wooden dock poles, fish it hard. Wood pole docks are best for bass. Wood docks are better because the algae that grows on the wood attract minnows. The minnows attract bigger fish which attract the bass. Steel poles are second best; aluminum is the least desirous, but still do not pass them up.

Flippin

There is not much to say about Flippin, the technique is simple. it is not easy; it is the hardest technique there is to master. You find a spot, either a hole in the weed mat, or a spot in the submerged trees.

Use a heavy enough jig to get through the cover and get to the bottom. Let the jig drop all the way to the bottom before you move it. Do not even put any tension on the line until it gets to the bottom.

Hop the jig up and down twice. Then let it sit still, do this again, then pull it out of the hole and drop it in another hole in the weed mat.

It is simple on the surface, but you must be precise with where you drop the jig. You will also struggle to pull fighting bass out of thick weeds they want to tangle up in. It is difficult to do well.

You need to use a stout rod and heavy line for Flippin. When you hook a nice bass in the heavy weeds, you do not want to go in after them. You need to pull them out of the weeds before they get tangled in the weeds.

The arky style jig heads are my favorite for Flippin. Most styles of jigs that are not round will work good for Flippin. You want to pull the jig through the weeds, with or without a bass on the end of the line.

Grubs

Grubs are great for jig fishing; you can use any style of jig head with any size and color of grub body and use it as a swim jig or a bottom bouncing jig. You can rig it Texas style to swim through weeds or use it on a jig head with a weed guard to fish it in timber or weeds.

Grubs are also great to rig with a Carolina rig setup.

Here is a great video from Bass Resources that will show you the best ways to rig grubs.

Tube Jigs

When tube jigs first came out in the mid 80's as a Gitzit jig, they seemed like a fad. They were so different and flashy. They appeared to be trying to appeal to the fisherman, instead of the fish. The amazing thing about these funny looking flashy jigs is that they catch Bass, and lots of them.

Tube jigs are a big deal now; they are up there with the most fished jigs there are. Average fisherman and many pros use them. Tube jigs were made to slide a long slim headed jig into the tube and push the hook eye through the tube. You were then ready to fish them as a finesse jig or a swimming jig.

Since the beginning, many ways to rig them have become popular and used by many fishermen. Although the weighted head inside the tube is by far still the most popular. The popularity continues because it is effective and catches bass.

Fishermen now rig them every way you can think of. They add rattles, and scents, and fish them through and around every type of structure there is. They are one of the most versatile jigs there is.

How far you push the head into the tube affects the action of the jig. If you push it in all the way to the end, the jig will fall faster and spin less. If you want the jig to fall slower and spin as it falls, do not push it all the way to the end of the tube. Stop it back and experiment with how the jig works.

The tube jig is great for fishing under docks. It is the best jig there is for shooting under docks like the video in the dock fishing section above shows you how to do.

Another cool thing you can do is to soak cotton balls in scent and pull off a small piece. Shove the piece of scented cotton into the tube to give off scent for many casts as it comes out of the cotton ball.

Also, if you put a small piece of alka seltzer into the tube, it gives off bubbles that also attracts fish.

Another tip is if you cut off the end of the tube and use it as a skirt for a spinnerbait, or a skirt for a jig.

Ways to rig a tube jig

- Rig it Texas style, like a worm, you can leave the hook point embedded into the inside of the opposite side of the tube.

- You can also push it through the opposite side of the tube and slide it up under the outside skin.
- You can also point the hook point, so it faces down. On the outside of the opposite side of the tube so it will not catch on anything.
- It works great as a weightless worm type rig. Put the hook eye inside the tube and the point on into the opposite side to be weedless. The extra weight of the bigger body of plastic makes it fall nice and slow like a weightless worm.
- A Carolina rigged tube is a great way to fish where you would fish a Carolina rigged worm. Here is a video on how to tie a Carolina rig.

Tubes are bulky and will catch weeds. They are not great for real thick weeds you need to pull the jig through. They work great for Flippin into pockets, as you would other jigs.

Tubes are one of the most versatile lures. You can catch everything from crappies and perch, to bass to stripers. They are also effective on many kinds of saltwater fish.

You can use your imagination about how you can fish a tube. Try anything you can think of it may catch fish; it may be the next latest thing.

[Here is another great video](#) to watch that will show you some alternate ways to rig a tube jig.

If you have not fished tube jigs, get some and try them, you will soon wonder why you have not tried them before.

Swim Jigs

Swim jigs are one of the most popular type of jig now. they are also very versatile. You can use swim jigs for almost any type of fishing and in most types of cover.

Swim jigs are easy to fish. Fishing a swim jig is like fishing a spinnerbait without the spinner. All the same techniques you use for spinnerbait fishing will work with swim jigs.

This is the easiest artificial lure you can fish. Most times they work best by casting and using a steady retrieve back to the boat. Use a ¼ to 3/8 oz jig head, a skinny to fatter tapered jig works best for swim jigs.

There are special jig heads that have a different placement of the jig eye. The eye on top gives it the right action to make the jig swim in a way that attracts fish. Other head styles will do the job also, but the swimming jig heads work best.

You want to have a smaller weed guard on a swim jig than you would have on a Flippin jig. Swim jigs come with fewer fiber pieces on the weed guard. If you use a non-swim jig head for a swim jig, cut down the weed guard so it is not so thick.

When you set the hook with a swim jig, the most effective way is to use a sweeping action. This set will pull the hook into the side of the fish's mouth and you will hook more fish.

This past winter I bought over 20 different brands of swim jig heads. They are similar but are all a bit different. I have tried many of them now and I like several of them. I have made several of my own special swim jigs from different heads.

I think my favorite so far is The Davis Baits Elite Swim Jig. I use a zoom super hog trailer or a sweet beaver trailer.

Here is a good video that will show you some excellent tweaks to get the most out of your swim jig fishing.

Trailers

Trailers for jigs always bring up varying opinions about what type and why you should use them.

I would say most of the time trailers are good if you are trying to make the jig perform a different way. If you want it to look bigger, or if you want it to fall slower, trailers are the best way to do that. If you want to impart more action into the jig, trailers are great. If you want to add a different color to the jig, trailers will do that.

If you want the jig to be the opposite of any of these things, do not use a trailer.

There are also several types of trailers you can use. I know no one who uses pork anymore; I have not for many years. I use either a plastic crawfish trailer or a grub with a twister tail.

You can use varying colors and sizes depending on what you want the effect to be.

Conclusion

The tackle you use for jig fishing will vary by choice. Many pros use baitcasters for jig fishing; I prefer to use spinning tackle, except for swim jigs. Whatever you feel comfortable with is the best thing to use for you.

Color varies with water temp and water clarity. You cannot go wrong if you use blue and or black, or combinations of them. Brown and orange are also a great choice. If you match the color of the jig to the food that the bass are eating, you will catch more bass.

Jigs are such a versatile lure they will catch Bass and most other types of fish. Depending on the style and fishing technique, you can fish jigs year-round with success. With small adjustments in technique and colors.

Tubes are popular because they catch fish. Tubes are also versatile. You can fish them in almost any cover and have many ways to rig them. If you have not fished tube jigs, get some and try them this year.

Try things you have never even heard of if you think they may work. You could hit on exactly what they want and catch a boatload of fish.

Many fishermen ignore jig fishing because it seems like too much trouble to learn. Some also think it is slow and not fun. It is like worm fishing in that if you have never tried it, you would never believe you could catch so many fish.

Do not use your trolling motor to troll and throw spinnerbaits at the shore all day. Learn to fish jigs and you will catch tons more fish.

Thank you so much for downloading and reading my book.

If you think this book has good info. Please go to the Amazon website and leave a review. Then more people will read this book and learn how to be a better fisherman.

BASS FISHING TIPS PLASTIC WORMS

How to catch Bass on worms

INTRODUCTION

Thank you for checking out my book. The tips and information in this book will make you a better bass fisherman.

Variations of the plastic worm have caught more Bass than any other bait. You can fish Plastic worms shallow or deep, fast, or slow. You can rig them in many ways, including weedless. You can fish them with or without weight. You can fish them in most every way you can think of, even sideways hooked in the middle, and still catch bass.

If you are a bass fisherman and you do not fish worms, you need to start. If you fish worms, you know how great they can be. This book is a great reference book for reading the best techniques and tips before you head out on the water. That way you can have all the best information fresh in your mind when you hit the lake.

If you are not a pro bass fisherman, you get to fish one or two days a week at most. When you have time to fish, you want to maximize your time on the water by catching the most bass every time you go out.

To do that, you need to have all the best tips and techniques fresh in your mind. So, when you need them, you will have them in your memory at a moment's notice with the confidence and technique you need.

You should have this book, and my other books on your phone and or tablet. Then you can do a quick read the night before you go fishing and have all the ideas and a plan in mind. If you do this, you can hit the lake and catch bass right away.

If you have questions. Contact me at. mailto:**steve@stevepease.net** or visit the site. Go to stevepease.net for more great reads and contact info.

Thanks for downloading and reading my book and go catch a boatful of bass.

TABLE OF CONTENTS

HISTORY

Plastic worms have been around for a long time. The first patent for a plastic or rubber style worm bait was in 1877. The bait was pure rubber, it was stiff, and few fishermen got excited about using them.

Nothing much happened until 1949. Nick Crème developed an experimental nylon mixture that gave a much more usable type of bait. Crème was making the worms in molds in his basement. He even had dried nightcrawlers mixed with cheese he was adding for scent. The Wiggle worm hit the market in 1951 and is still made today under the name Scoundrel.

In 1967 Tom Mann introduced the Jelly worm with a soft and realistic feel, along with a choice of many colors. That is when worm fishing took off.

In 1972 a company called Mister Twister came out with the curly tail worm. It added a whole new dimension to worms and the world of soft plastic baits. Now there was a worm that added its own action.

I use Mister Twister curly tail grubs for trailers. I use them for jigs, spinnerbaits, and even for bait bodies for several types of lures.

Today there are worms made with ribbon tails and curly tails and worms made from actual fish. There is no color or shape or action of worm you cannot get now. They all work sometimes. But the old Crème, Mann's, and Mister Twister baits are still going strong, and are still some of the most effective.

There are now close to 100 different manufacturers of plastic worms. Many of which are extraordinarily successful at their business. There are 3 main reasons that worms are so successful. They catch bass, they are inexpensive, and you can fish them in cover or no cover. They are one of a few baits you can fish anywhere bass swim.

TACKLE

There are a lot of choices in tackle for worm fishing, and bass fishing. Each type has its place, and most of it is a matter of choice. What I like may differ from what you like for a particular fishing. It is all good and depends on what you prefer.

Reels

The reel you choose determines the rod you use. There are differences in rods, you also will have to choose. I like spinning gear. I have a better feel for what is going on with the worm. And it is easier to cast weightless worms on a spinning set up than it is a baitcasting set up.

I prefer to use a baitcasting rod and reel for fast fishing baits. Baits like spinnerbaits and crankbaits and swim jigs. Many fishermen prefer a bait casting set up for worms. Which is fine, it is something you will have to see what works better for you. There is no right or wrong answer to this question.

Rods

The choice of a rod starts with spinning or baitcasting as your main choice. From there you must decide what weight of line and the action you are looking for in the rod.

I like to use a Shimano worm and jig rod with a good backbone and a fast tip, so I have a good feel of the worm or jig. Sometimes a bass will hit a worm with subtle hit, and you will miss it if you have less feel of the bait.

If you choose a spinning system or a bait casting system. Make sure you get a rod that gives you the power to pull the bass out of thick cover. While still giving you good feel on the end of the line.

Line

The line you choose is also a matter of preference, what feels good to you. I used Trilene XT and Trilene XL for many years and I have no issues with the line.

There are many other choices on the market, with braided and Fluorocarbon lines. Once again, nothing wrong with any of them. I prefer to use fluorocarbon on my spinning rod for worms, and I use braid for my bait casters for spinnerbaits and crankbaits. I like the fluorocarbon because it has less memory than mono, and I use the braid because it does not break and has no memory.

If you have a line you like and works well, use it. Once again there is no right or wrong online choice. Many pros still use monofilament line for many types of lures and techniques.

Hooks

Most worm hooks are for Texas rigging of plastic worms. There are 2 types that are most used, they are a straight hook with 2 90-degree bends below the eye. This style of hook makes it easy to Texas rig the worm. You thread the hook through and turn it around to push back through the bait.

Here is a good video that shows you how to rig the worm onto the hook for a Texas rig. You can do the line and weight differently, but this is the best way to put the hook into the worm for fishing in heavy weeds.

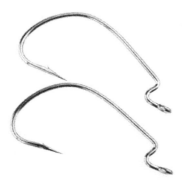

The other type is a straight hook with or without some keeper on the other side of the eye. It may be a metal screw shaped wire you screw into the end of the worm. Or it may be a straight pointed piece of steel with barbs on it. Both are to hold the worm straight when you hook the worm and while you are fishing it.

I like the Mister Twister keeper hooks better because the worm slides off the keeper better. It is easier on the worms than the screw in keepers and the hook goes through the worm and into the bass mouth easier. The keeper style hooks are available with or without weight. It does not tear the worm up as much so you can catch more than one bass on a worm.

There are a lot of variations of these types of hooks. The makers have different ideas of the best way to make them. Different offsets, and special hooks for wacky style worms. But most are variations of the above-mentioned hooks.

There are hooks with weights molded onto the shanks that also are amazingly effective. You can make it overly complicated with all the options out there but try and keep it as simple as you can.

Weights

As for worm weights, there is a plethora of choices in this area. I prefer the hooks with the weights molded on the shank. Many fishermen still use the bullet sinkers on the line above the hook. For some rigs they are best, but I like the weight on the hooks. They catch fewer weeds.

You can use the bullet weights, you can use the weighted hooks, you can even use regular jig heads as worm hooks. One thing that makes worms so awesome is that there are no limits on how you can fish them. There are also hundreds of ways you can rig them to catch bass.

GENERAL TIPS

Here is a good set of tips if you are a bank fisherman. The key is keeping it simple and portable, which goes against most types of bass fishing. Bass fishermen have tons of lures and accessories to use with the lures. If you are like me, you have tons of tackle and you bring most of it with you in case you need it. You want to make sure you have plenty in case something is working better than anything else.

When being mobile is important. Carrying the least amount of tackle, you need is critical, while still having everything you need. I read a great article and I want to share this information with you. What you need to carry with you for bank worm fishing. One pack of ribbon tail worms in your favorite color. One pack of floating worms your favorite color one pack a stick worm. Then all you need is one package of size 2/0 or 3/0 keeper worm hooks, with and without weights. 1/8th oz. work well.

1/8th ounce worm weights might seem too lightweight for some of you. The reason is when you are fishing from the bank you are almost always going to be fishing in or around and through some debris. The lighter weight will get your worms down but will let it fall slower to entice more strikes.

Strategy for fishing like this will start with the Texas rigged ribbon tail worm. Search the area in front of you. Cast out 45° to the right side Make the worm drop and hop or drag it back, feeling the depth and structure under the water.

On the next cast, cast a little further to the right repeat the same retrieve and work your way towards the shore. Make sure your last cast is close to the shore; sometimes those nice bass are right next to the shore.

Then cast out 45° to the left do the same, working your way into the shore. Once you reach the shore cast the next series straight in front of you and work 45° to each side.

After you finish the entire area in front of you with the ribbon tail worm, switch to a wacky rig Senko. To fish the Senko, remember where you found structure when you were fishing with a ribbon tail rig. Then throw the Senko at those areas and be ready on the drop to get bit.

Most of your strikes on the wacky rig will be when your worm is dropping with a slack line. When it reaches the bottom give it a twitch, if no bites, hop the worm and stop it, then hop it again and stop.

After you have fished the area with the Senko worm. The next option is to put on a weightless floating worm and cover the same area. Fishing right below the surface. This technique can be fantastic if the bass are active. With floating worms, they seem to work well with colors you would not use for worms most times. Bright colors. Like pink, orange white and even fluorescent green can be amazingly effective.

Next try a senko style stick worm rigged Texas style. Fish it like a straight tail worm with same fancast technique.

In low light conditions with overcast skies. The bass will be tight to cover, and the floating bright color worm can be effective. Make long casts and dance the worm under the surface by twitching it and drag it a little way pause shake it more.

Using these techniques with these three types of worms. Fishing from a bank should be amazingly effective. And you can cover a lot of area and catch the most bass possible from that area.

A good general tip on how to fish for the day. If you get out in the morning before or as the sun is coming up, fish close to shore with a black worm. Hit all the good structure looking for the good spots you can find.

When the worm hits the water allow the worm to drop on a slackline. When the worm touches the bottom is when you get most of your strikes. If you feel the thump point the Rod toward the worm. Take up the slack and set the hook hard. If the bass is on set the hook one more time to make sure it is embedded in his mouth.

One of the best general tips I can give you is. Do not fish a worm to fast most of the time. Sometimes it is extremely hard to be patient you want to catch fish but if you slow down you will catch more fish.

If you think a bass has picked up the worm, set the hook. If there is a fish, you got them. If there is no fish, you have nothing to lose. One thing about worm fishing on a Texas rigged worm, you will not catch fish if you do not set the hook. Always set the hook twice.

SEASONAL

Plastic worms will catch bass any time of year. There are some different things you can do to make them better in the different seasons. Do these things and it will have you catching more bass all year. Water temperature, water clarity, and cover are the keys to determining how to fish in different seasons.

Spring

In the spring when the water is cold, below 60 degrees, the key is slow. When the water temp gets above 60, you can try quicker and more erratic retrieves to get bass to strike.

Floating rigs and wacky rigs are both great spring bass baits. We will go over these rigs later in the book.

In the spring stick worms are amazingly effective, they are one of the simplest yet effective ways to catch more Bass. One of the great things about a stick worm is that it is almost impossible to fish them wrong.

A Senko or Senko type worm is one of the best baits to use in many situations. If there are bass close to you where you are fishing, they will hit on a Senko.

When the water temperature is cold, a Carolina rig is one of the best ways to use a stick worm to catch more Bass.

If you are fishing bedding bass, a Carolina rig is also great for that. You can drag it around through the beds and entice those bass to hit.

A Texas rigged five-inch Senko is a great search bait for post spawn bass. The ones that are cruising the flats looking for bluegill beds.

Docks and pontoon boats also attract a lot of bass in the spring; a wacky rig is a great way to fish those areas. Stay alert, most of the strikes will come as the worm sinks while using a weightless worm rig.

Summer

In the summer, a wacky rig is a great choice. Fishing bigger worms for most situations is better as the water warms. You can use up to a 10-inch worm in the summer. Fish it in the same areas you would a smaller worm in the colder water conditions.

Bill Seibel from Outdoor guide magazine. Says when the water gets warm and the sun is hot, "nothing catches bass like a big worm." He considers a big worm over 9 inches.

The most common variety of the big worm is the ribbon tail worms, you fish them by dragging them along the bottom. The swimming action of the worm's ribbon tail swims along and gets the big bass to bite.

If you are fishing with a big worm, you need to wait about 2 seconds after you feel the thump before you set the hook. Research has shown when bass hit a big worm. They hit it in the middle; they then suck it in 2 more times before they eat the whole worm.

You only need 3 colors of worms for the big ones. Plum is the best in stained water and cloudy conditions. Green pumpkin is best in clear water with sunny skies, and red shad is the best all-around color for most places.

Fall

One of the best worm rigs for fall is a big Senko wacky rig; fish it slow and on the bottom. Fall fishing is when the bass are trying to load up for the winter. They will attack everything you throw at them sometimes.

I love fishing docks and the remaining weed beds. There are good weeds and not so good weeds. If you find an area of cabbage weed in your lake, fish it, there are bass in that weed bed, do not overlook cabbage weeds. Cabbage weed is also called curly leaf pondweed.

Longtime professional bass fisherman Shaw Grigsby has techniques he uses in the fall. When the fishing gets tough, he uses his technique around structure. Especially docks and bridges. Talking about the shaky head rig.

When he uses the shaky head method on docks, he starts at the first pole from the shoreline. Work your way out to the outside edges.

Bridges often cut the middle of creeks and streams. The pilings funnel the bass into certain areas. This makes them easier to find. They will sit on the backside of the current breaking object, or anything else deflecting the current.

Shaw uses a 3/16-ounce, 1/8 ounce, or ¼ ounce shaky head jigs. He leans more towards more aggressive worms, not finesse worms.

Grigsby also says to keep your retrieve simple. Drag it along the bottom until you hit a piece of cover. Shake it in place a couple of times, and before you reel it back to the boat, stop and let it sit for a time, then bring it back.

Another Grigsby's favorite is the wacky rig he also fishes on docks. He fishes his wacky rig little different than many people. Put a 1/16-ounce nail weight inside the worm in the middle. He says this allows him to get the worm down to the bottom faster so he can fish the area faster. But he also adds. When you are fishing the wacky rig do not fish it too fast. Lift it and let it sink back to the bottom, then hop it a few inches at a time.

Winter

One of the most important things to remember when fishing for bass in the winter. They will not move extremely far or fast for a lure; you must slow way down. You are better off taking 10 casts on one piece of structure if you think there are bass there, instead of casting and moving a lot.

The bass will stay close to structure. Bass in the winter also seem to like steep Banks more than gentle drop offs. They also like to suspend off the steep Banks. Stair stepping the worm down the steep drop offs is amazingly effective in the winter.

As for worm fishing in the winter, it is a good idea to use a small wacky worm; they seem to work great on winter bass. The stick bait or Senko type baits are the best winter worms. Even if you are fishing them Texas rigged or on a jig head, you should use a stick bait.

The tackle changes in the winter. You will want to go down to 8-to-10-pound line and use lighter weights. More like you are crappie fishing than bass fishing. When you cast be alert as the worm drops, many strikes come as the worm falls to the bottom.

WHERE TO FISH

As for where to fish, there is no limit on where you can fish plastic worms. That is why they catch more Bass than any other Lure. We will go over some of the places where they work best, and the best techniques to fish them in those places.

Light cover

Light cover will cover everything from open water to sparse weed growth. You can fish most any rig in light cover. All the way from an open hook jig head with the worm or grub. Or any plastic bait. You can fish them Texas style. Or split shot rig, drop shot rig, Carolina rigged, wacky rigged, shaky head or even a floating rig.

My favorite way to fish light cover like sparse weeds is a bare hook jig with a curly tail grub, or a **wild eye swimbait**.

Heavy cover

For heavy cover, meaning thick weeds or flooded timber, flipping is the best way to go. Flipping with a jig also works with a worm. Instead of flipping, try a floating worm dragged across the tops of the weeds. This can also be amazingly effective.

Lily pads

One cool thing to do when fishing Lily pads. If there is no wind, look over the area of Lily pads and look for any movement of the Lily pads. One thing for sure in weeds that thick. There is no way a bass can move through the Lily pad stems without bumping them and moving them.

If they bump the stems, it moves the leaves on the surface. So, look for the leaves moving in a way that looks like something below is bumping into them.

Another way to check Lily pads for signs of life is stop and listen. A good patch of Lily pads will have a lot of insects. Insects land on the surface and on the Lily pads. And if you listen you should be able to hear bluegills eating the bugs off the surface. They make a slight popping sound or snapping sound, it is a very definite sound if you have heard it before. If there are small bluegills in the lily pads, there will also be bass.

Another thing to remember about Lily pads. If you get a bass hooked and he gets tangled up in the stems of the Lily pads do not fight it too much. Move your boat as close as you can over top of where the bass is and work him loose. If you fight and yank from a distance. You will lose them. Lily pads are tough and strong. Your chances of breaking a stem are almost impossible without losing the fish.

Docks

There are a lot of different baits that work well when fishing docks. One of my favorites is a weightless worm cast up under the dock. Let it sit still for up to a minute, then twitch it back to the boat. Make sure along the way you hit every post you can, and when you hit the post let it suspend and sink.

Docks are one of my favorite places to fish anywhere on the lake and almost any time of year. They will always hold fish, sometimes they are not as big but there are always fish around docks. The main reason docks are always holding fish. Because docks always have smaller fish and minnows around. The key to finding bass is finding the food source, find the food source, and find the bass.

TYPES OF WORMS

One thing that is important with most types of worm fishing. When you cast always let your bait fall straight to the bottom before engaging the reel. It is not natural looking if the bait drops and moves in an arc movement. Always watch the line when it is dropping, many hits come on the drop.

If the worm gets to the bottom without a fish picking it up, raise the rod tip up 45° and reel up your line so it has a slight bow. The object is to have a little slack in the line so the fish will not feel the tension. But have the line tight enough so you can detect any bites, and when you set the hook, it goes into the fish's mouth.

Straight

A straight tail worm is by far the most versatile worm of any. They sink quicker than other types of worms and they come through weeds well. Larry Nixon long time pro bass fisherman says there is never a bad time to use a straight tail worm.

Curly tail

Curly tail worms are the best when you fish vegetation. Especially lily pads, they have a realistic swimming action.

Senko

A senko worm or stick worm as many people call them. Is the basic 4- or 5-inch straight worm great for catching bass almost anywhere. These worms are not tapered like a normal straight tail worm.

Pro bass fisherman Brent Ehrler said, "if the water is wet and bass live in it you can catch them on a Senko."

The parts of casting and fishing a Senko worm. First part is the splash, bass react to the splash. They will come and investigate the splash, after it hits the water leave it set, do not move it at all for up to a minute. That will allow the worm to spin and twist its way to the bottom. Often, they will pick it up and eat it as it falls.

After the worm reaches the bottom and you let it sit for a time. You then want to make it twitch. A slight twitch is what you want, you do not want to move the worm. Then let it set motionless again for a while.

Raise your Rod tip to lift the worm off the bottom and let it drop back again. Do this a few more times and bring it back to the boat. People ask how long you let it sit. You can leave it set for even up to two minutes or longer depending on what the fish tell you they want.

Ribbon Worm

The ribbon worm has a long thin piece of soft plastic behind the body that gives the worm a swimming action. As it moves through the water the tail swims back and forth. Ribbon worms are good to use in areas where an injured baitfish is what you are trying to portray.

CREATURE BAITS

Creature baits are all the other baits that are not worms. Twister tail grubs, lizards, crayfish, anything that is not a worm. There are also several other types of insects like grasshoppers and bees.

Grubs

The category of grubs covers most type of soft body type creatures. They will work with lead head jigs and exposed hooks or Texas rigged. They can be used in most types of situations you find. You can even add a spinner above them like with Mr. Twister beetle spins.

The consensus on color for grubs seems to go with lighter colors. White, yellow, chartreuse, motor oil, pumpkinseed, salt-and-pepper, and smoke are the most used. Some of them are even somewhat translucent with flecks of metal flake in them to help reflect lighter.

Lizards

For creature baits lizards are up there at the top. Lizards are used by all top bass fishermen. Using lizards during spawning time is a fantastic approach. Bass hate lizards anywhere near their spawning beds. Lizards are notorious for stealing bass eggs. The bass know it, so anytime they see a lizard they will attack out of protection.

Texas rigged lizards. Cast past the nest then drag it into and through the nest. This will often cause an attack from the female. Dragging lizards along ledges and points are also very productive. Many other rigs work well for lizards. Drop shot rigs, Carolina rings, and even swimming a lizard can be amazingly effective. Weightless Texas rigged is also great.

Crayfish

Crayfish are also one of the best bass baits you can use because it is one of the bass favorite foods.

COLOR SELECTION

Choosing the right color to use for plastic worms can be very daunting. If you walk down the aisle of any Bass fishing store you will see endless numbers of colors. Most bass fisherman look at the plastic worms to start, and they buy colors they like. These might not be the same colors that the bass like, many colored lures are to attract fishermen not fish.

Just because you know this is true does not mean you can stop it. It happens all the time. I buy different colored lures because they look cool, it has nothing to do with how the fish think about color. The next thing that can happen is you find one color you like. And you try nothing else. This can also be bad even though some colors will work most of the time. You will still limit yourself if you do not keep an open mind.

Sometimes a subtle difference in color can make a big difference to the bass. I have seen it happen to me. I was fishing a light grape colored worm and was catching fish. I caught a nice fish that ripped the worm. I put on a darker colored purple that was not much different. I could not catch anything on it. I changed back to the other color and started catching fish again. They were not much different but enough for the bass to see.

Here are a few good rules to go by

On sunny days in Clear water the best colors are watermelon, watermelon red, pumpkin, and plum.

On sunny days in darker water. June bug, black with red glitter, and black with blue glitter are good colors.

On cloudy days in Clear water. Green pumpkin, green pumpkin with purple, and green pumpkin with blue are some of the top colors.

On cloudy days in dirty water, black, black, and blue, and dark blue are effective.

Dirty water

Determining the difference between clear and dirty water. It depends a lot on what is available and what is considered clear water. In some places that can mean weed lines at 30 feet deep, Clear water in other places can mean weed lines at 4 feet deep. The same thing goes for dirty water. Some places it can be visibility of less than a foot, and sometimes visibility of less than 4 feet.

As you can see from the previous list, in darker water bass prefer darker colors. This seems to work in both sunny and cloudy conditions. One of the best colors for worms I have ever used is an electric grape. Dark purple is also particularly good in clear water. Most of the lakes I fish, the water is clear. These colors have worked well for many years.

Tom Mann once said if you do not know what color to use you can never go wrong with a black worm. I found this to be true, even in the clear lakes I have also found black is always a good choice. The darker June bug colors with different colors mixed in with it are also good, and dark blues also work well.

The most important thing to think of in dirtier water is contrast. The contrast between the worm and the sky in the background will make the worm easier to see if it is a darker color.

Stained water

For stained water, you are kind of in the middle of the clear and dirty. Most stained water lakes have a dark or rusty tint, caused from springs running into the lake or from weeds coloring the water. They are not dirty unless it is run off from heavy rain.

Good colors to use in stained water are kind of the same as in dirty water but a little lighter. Some lighter colored blues. Lighter colored purples, and several shades of green work well.

How dark the sky is also can make a big difference, the cloudier or darker the sky the darker the worm you want to use. Bass have their eyes on the top of their head, so they are always looking up. If you look up towards the sky from underwater the more contrast there is, the easier it is to see the worm.

Clear water

In Clear water more translucent colors work better. Translucent colors such as watermelon and pumpkin blend in with the surroundings. But they are highly effective at enticing bass. Watermelon or pumpkin-colored baits with flakes are also great for enticing because of the flash.

When it is cloudy or darker and you are fishing in Clear water darker hues of green and Brown are more effective.

Many pro bass fishermen have very defined colors they use, and they try to keep them as simple as possible. Gary Mumphrey, touring Bass Pro likes to keep his choices simple. In clear or lightly stained water he uses green pumpkin. In stained water he uses June bug, in dark stained water he uses black blue or some other variation of black.

One thing nice about a strategy like this. Keeping it simple and giving the bass something, they like. It is much easier than trying to decide from hundreds of different colors.

Here are the choices of another all-time top bass fishing Pro Bill Dance

Black, black works well in any color or clarity of water and it looks like some of the bass's favorite food, it looks like a leech.

Green pumpkin. Green pumpkin is another great all-around color, great for lizards, and worms.

June bug, the dark purple color with green flakes works good in clear to dark water. "Dance says "I often use it rather than black when I want a little sparkle".

Pumpkin seed. Pumpkin seed came out in the late 80s and took the bass world by storm. This color is still great and was the basis for many similar colors that work well.

Watermelon, it is hard to beat the green color in Clear water, a little bit of glitter makes it a little better.

Black grape and basic blue are great colors from the 70s. They still work well and are never a bad choice.

So, do not get too hung up on color. Stick to the basics and the guidelines listed above. If you do you will have no problem catching bass on plastic worms.

WORM RIGS

Here is a great video about how to rig several different plastic baits.

Texas Rig

How to set up a Texas rigged bait.

The tackle you use for fishing Texas rigged worms and any other worm is a lot of personal preference. Many guys prefer a bait casting tackle. I prefer spinning tackle for fishing worms and most soft plastics. It is easier to control and you have a better feel for what the Lure is doing.

As with all worm rigs the Texas rig is no different. You want to use the smallest weight you can get away with, while still getting to the depth you need. One of my favorite ways to fish with a Texas rigged worm is using a stick bait worm Texas rigged with no weight. It is not a floating rig, but it works like one. I cast it to the spot and work it through the tops of the weeds and around structure. I have caught hundreds of bass on this rig.

Cast it out and let it set for 30 seconds to a minute. Then twitch it through the tops of the weeds, this is a great way to fish medium to thick submerged weed beds.

If you think a fish picks up the worm. Real down and take up the slack and set the hook hard. When you hook the fish, it is a good idea to set the hook one more time to make sure it is through the jaw or lip.

If you set the hook and there is no fish pull the bait back in fix it. Then cast again. It is likely that you messed up the worm when you set the hook, leaving it sit there will not get the fish to strike it again.

The Texas rig is the most used rig for fishing plastic worms, but it is also one of the most effective. A great thing about the Texas rig is you can fish it in heavy cover, and it does not get hung up as much. You can drag it through almost anything.

Setting up the Texas rigged worm can and will work several different ways. My favorite way is with a #2 or # 3 worm hook that has the 90° bend at the top. Rigging it that way makes it easy to get straight.

Texas rigged worms

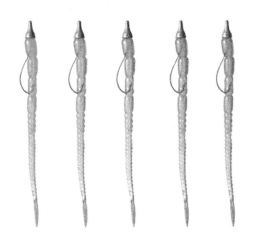

My second favorite way to rig it is with the Mr. Twister keeper hooks. Or one of the other keeper hooks that has the screw in piece or the strait barbed piece to hold the worm on.

You can set up a Texas rig with any hook you want. You can use a standard jig head. You can use a shaky head jig. You can use a straight worm hook, or any of the many types of specialty worm hooks that are available.

To do the Texas rigged worm you push the hook through the top part of the worm and bring it out. Turn it over and push it back through the worm till comes out the other side. Then you slide the worm forward and bring it back, so the hook tip is in the worm.

I still sometimes rig it the old-fashioned way. Push the hook through almost to the other side of the worm and stop. That leaves the hook point buried in the worm, like the picture above.

As far as retrieves for Texas rigged worm. You are unlimited on how you can retrieve it. You can drag it, hop it, swim it, or any other retrieve, they all work well with the Texas rig setup. The one time I would not use this setup is if you are fishing open flats where there is little cover. I would use a worm on a jig head and leave the hook exposed; you will catch more fish that way.

Texas rig setup is not only for worms. You can hook all soft plastics this way and make them highly effective for fishing almost any cover.

Here is another great video about Texas rigging soft plastics.

Watch the videos above if you need more instruction.

Split shot Rig

The split shot rig is my second favorite type of worm or soft plastic rig. It is like a Carolina rig, but it is easier to fish and is easier to set up.

The way you set up this rig is to tie the line to a hook. Whatever type of hook you choose. Hook on your soft plastic, you can rig it Texas style or leave the hook bare depending on where you are fishing.

Then you put a small split shot sinker 18 to 24 inches up the line. One important thing about the sinker is make sure you use one that is round without the tabs on it. Otherwise, the tabs get caught on the weeds and other cover. Or use slider weights.

This approach also works well in places where most people would not fish. The more boring areas, open flats Sandy bottom areas, and points with little structure. This technique also works well on shallow flats. It works great on sloping points, sandbars, boat launch ramps and sandy points.

The best worm I found to use this method for is a 4-inch twister tail grub. Throw it up near docks and other cover and drag it or hop it back.

Drop shot Rig

The drop shot rig is a popular new rig. It is most effective in water temperatures below 55° where the fish are in deep water. The best baits for drop shot are 4-inch plastics.

The rig comprises a heavy sinker tied to the end of the line with the hook 10 inches to 4 feet above the sinker. This rig is good for deep water. It also works well in shallower water if you have new weed growth. It is very versatile, and you can really use it anywhere. Do not be afraid to try it in any situation.

Video about how to set up a drop shot rig.

Carolina Rig

The Carolina rig for soft plastic has been used for a long time. It is a well proven way to rig plastic. A Carolina rig is a set up with a weight that runs along the bottom. The bait runs on a leader above the weight dragging behind. Works well if you want to keep your bait at a certain level off the bottom over large area.

I used to use the Carolina rig a lot when fishing flats with sparse weeds or sand bottom and it works well in those areas. I now use the split shot rig, or a drop shot rig for most of those areas, it is easier to setup, and easier to fish. One big advantage to using a Carolina rig is you can cover a lot of water fast.

Good tips for fishing a Carolina rig
Here is a good video for rigging a Carolina rig.

Wacky Rig

The wacky rig is another one of my favorites, the reason is because it works well in many areas. I read a trick a few years ago about using tiny zip ties on the middle of the worms to hold the hook.

I ordered some O rings for the wacky rig; they work well also. Otherwise, the zip ties work well. Depending on the strength of the O-rings I may use the zip ties. I got the o ring wacky installer that Jimmy Houston uses in this video and it works great. The advantage to hooking the worm like this instead of going through the worm. Is the worms will hold up better without the hook tearing it and because the hook is in line with the worm, you will hook more strikes. You can even use 2 o rings and do not hook it through the worm at all.

There are several other ways you can rig a wacky worm. There is even a new jig head that has a loop on it, and you put the worm through the loop. That way you can have a weighted wacky worm, I have not tried it, but it looks cool.

There is a new Senko style worm out that has the o ring molded inside the worm. You hook it through the worm and through the o ring.

The most basic way to rig it is hooking the hook right through the center part of the worm. The bad thing about doing it that way is it tears the worm, and the worms are good for only one hook set.

You can use about any kind of worm for a wacky rig; most common and the best are the Senko style or other stick worm. Most of these worms are salt impregnated. Which gives them extra weight, they fall better because they are heavier. You can change it by adding nail weights into one or the other end of the worm to allow it to fall different.

Shaky head

A shaky head rig is a jig head with A keeper mechanism to hold the worm on the end. And then it is rigged Texas style and dragged or hopped along the bottom.

The shaky part comes from stopping and shaking your Rod tip. This shakes the line and the jig wiggles. That wiggles the tail of the worm a little bit which is incredibly good for enticing bass.

The shaky head rig does not have to get shaken. You can drag it, hop it, or swim it. You can fish it much like any other worm rig. The name that is given to it because of the set up in the way it gets fished.

You want to use a floating worm for shaky head rig. Best way to tell if a worm floats is to see if their salt in it. Most salt impregnated worms do not float. Although one salt impregnated worm I know does, the zoom trick worm.

When you are looking at jig heads to use, there are two ways to have the eye on the jig head, 90° or 60°. The 90° shakes more but gets hung up more, the 60° shakes less but is much easier to fish in thick cover.

The best time to use the shaky head is when fishing is the toughest. After a cold front, cold water etc. It is a terribly slow fishing technique.

Here is a video about fishing the shaky head.

Floating

The floating rig is a setup that uses a floating worm, a leader of line, a swivel, and then connected to your regular line. Floating worms will spin around as you retrieve it to the boat. So, the swivel is on there, so you do not get your line all twisted.

Use a light wire hook with a floating worm. Use this for fishing through the tops of weeds, under docks or in and around other structure.

This retrieve for a floating rig is to twitch it and move it and stop. Twitch it again, stop again, and continue doing that through the structure.

One other thing that is different about the floating rig. You will generally use bright almost fluorescent-colored worms. Many of the floating worms for the floating rig, are great in the spring and on cloudy or overcast days.

When setting the hook on a floating rig always wait a second or two before you set the hook to allow the bass to eat it. When they take the worm, they will take it from the side and stop. They will suck in on it two more times, that is when you want to set the hook.

There are several other types of worm rigs. I am sure they catch bass, but these are the most common, the most used, and the most effective

CONCLUSION

Worms and soft plastic baits are some of the most successful baits to use for catching bass. There are several main ways to rig soft plastic to be the most effective.

Rubber and plastic worms have been around for a long time. They were not popular or amazingly effective at first. Not until the softer more lifelike plastics came on the scene. And now they can also be any color.

If you use spinning or casting equipment, is up to you. Some fishermen prefer bait casting equipment for worm fishing, some prefer spinning equipment. The best rods are ones for worm fishing. They are medium to medium heavy with a fast tip for extra feel.

In the spring you want to fish slow, stick worms are great in spring in most areas, fished Texas rigged or wacky style.

In the summer you can use bigger worms to catch bigger bass. Wacky style still works well. Try to keep your fishing simple.

In the fall, the wacky style still works well. Fish the docks and any remaining weed beds. The shaky head method is great in colder water also.

In winter, the key is to fish slow. Fish close to any remaining structure, and along big drop-offs and steep banks.

Light cover and flat, use the split shot rig or a bare hook rig.

In heavy cover use a floating rig or flipping.

When fishing docks, use a weightless worm or split shot rig, hit posts of docks. Start at inside or outside edges and work to the other.

As far as color goes, try to keep it simple. In clear water conditions, use watermelon, pumpkin or plum. In dark or dirty water, use June bug, black, blue, or combinations of blacks or combinations of blues.

There are many types of worm rigs. The most popular are the Texas rig, the Wacky rig, and the split shot rig and the floating rig. They can work in different places and for different fishing.

Worms and plastic baits are very versatile. They can be use in almost all fishing situations and types of water and structure.

Read this book before heading out on the lake and have all the best tips in your mind and ready for catching bass.

*If you think this book had good information, and you have a couple of minutes. I would be grateful if you would go to the **Amazon website** and put up a short review about the book.*

Thanks for downloading and reading my book and go catch a boatful of bass.

Thanks again

Check out my book site for other good books.
Stevepease. net

Here are a few other books covering the things you need to know to be the best bass fisherman you can be.

Bass Fishing tips for fishing a New Lake

Do you want to know how to go on a new lake and catch bass like you fish it all the time? One of the toughest things for weekend Bass fisherman is knowing where to find fish. It gets harder when you are fishing a lake you have not fished before.

Bass Fishing Tips Spinner baits

Learn to fish spinnerbaits with confidence and the right technique. This will make you a better bass fisherman. Spinnerbaits along with crankbaits are the search lures. These are the lures you fish with to find the active and aggressive fish on any body of water.

Bass Fishing Tips: Where when and how to fish crankbaits

Crank baits are one of the most popular baits for bass fishing. Almost all bass fishermen use crankbaits and have for many years. We use them because they catch fish. Knowing the right techniques will make you more successful with crank baits.

Bass Fishing Tips, Bass fishing with jigs

You can ask tournament fisherman who fish for bass. From North to South and East to West. They will tell you can and will catch bigger bass with Jigs than you will fishing with worms. You may not catch as many, but they will be bigger.

*If you think this book has good information, and you have a couple of minutes. I would be grateful if you would go to the **Amazon website** and put up a short review about the book.*

OTHER BOOKS YOU MAY BE INTERESTED IN

Kayak fishing, how to get started and set up your boat

Kayak fishing is growing in popularity by leaps and bounds for many good reasons. Most of the reasons for the popularity are practical reasons that make sense.

Northern Pike Fishing

Why you should read this book

This book does not cover every aspect of Pike fishing. I wrote this book so you can take it with you or read it the night before hitting the water. This is so you can have all the best tips and techniques fresh in your mind. It an easy read which will help you remember all the best ways to catch Pike when you get in the boat.

I read a saying that makes me think of catching Pike. It said, "God let me catch a fish today so big that when I talk about it later, I don't even have to exaggerate its size." This is a possibility when fishing for Pike almost anywhere they roam. Every cast you throw in Pike waters could get you hooked on the biggest freshwater fish you will ever catch.

Made in the USA
Coppell, TX
15 February 2023

12901760R00128